KAY FISKER

DANISH FUNCTIONALISM AND
BLOCK-BASED HOUSING

KAY FISKER

DANISH FUNCTIONALISM AND
BLOCK-BASED HOUSING

Andrew Clancy and Colm Moore

First published in 2022 by Lund Humphries

Lund Humphries
Huckletree Shoreditch
The Alphabeta Building
18 Finsbury Square
London, EC2A 1AH
UK
www.lundhumphries.com

Kay Fisker: Danish Functionalism and Block-based Housing © Andrew Clancy and Colm Moore, 2022

All rights reserved

978-1-84822-405-6

A Cataloguing-in-Publication record for this book is available from the British Library. All rights reserved. No part of this publication may be reproduced, stored in a retrieval system or transmitted in any form or by any means, electrical, mechanical or otherwise, without first seeking the permission of the copyright owners and publishers. Every effort has been made to seek permission to reproduce the images in this book. Any omissions are entirely unintentional, and details should be addressed to the publishers.

Andrew Clancy and Colm Moore have asserted their right under the Copyright, Designs and Patent Act, 1988, to be identified as the Authors of this Work.

Front cover Dronningegarden facade
Project editor Anna Norman
Design Clancy Moore, with additional typesetting by Binomi Design
Essays editor Eleanor Beaumont
Set in Akzidenz-Grotesk
Printed in Estonia

About this book

This book documents a number of seminal housing projects by Kay Fisker. It was first published as part of the involvement of Clancy Moore Architects in the Biennale Architettura 2018 at the invitation of curators Yvonne Farrell, Shelley McNamara and Hugh Campbell. Since then we have worked with Val Rose at Lund Humphries to augment this work with additional essays and reflections.

The primary research in terms of measured drawings was carried out by the M. Arch Economy Housing Studio Unit at Queen's University, Belfast, led by Clancy Moore Architects in 2016. A big thank you to our students there for their dedication in the production of the drawings and photographs featured here – it was a joy to work with you.

We would like to thank all those who contributed and in particular to Job Floris, Martin Soberg, and Tony Fretton. Thanks to Eleanor Beaumont for editing and critique. Thanks also to Prof. Greg Keefe and Prof. Michael McGarry at Queen's University Belfast. Most of all, thanks to Val Rose and Anna Norman at Lund Humphries for their infinite patience and ever-positive messages.

Authors:
Andrew Clancy and Colm Moore

Guest essays:
Job Floris, Tony Fretton, Poul Sverrild and Martin Soberg

Guest editing:
Eleanor Beaumont

Graphic design:
Matthew Kernan and David Magennis

Student contributors (drawings, photography, texts):
Kathryn Dowse, Brendan George, Alice Gordon,
Brendan Holbeach, Matthew Kernan, Magdalena Kisiel,
Matthew Lucas, Stephen McClelland, Mark Scott
Darragh Sherry, Jamie Sloan, Philippa Southall
Natalie Taylor, Darragh Tracey

Additional photography: Jens Seier, Job Floris, Colm Moore

Vestersøhus. Photo: Jens Seier.

Dronningegården. Photo: Jens Seier.

Contents

8	**Between Strategy and Detail:** Kay Fisker and the Conditions of Life *Andrew Clancy and Colm Moore*
18	**Kay Fisker's Classical Principles for Modern Housing** *Martin Søberg*
28	**An Outline of Danish Social Housing History** *Poul Sverrild*
30	**Dronningegården and Kay Fisker's Continuum** *Job Floris*
38	**Building Study 1: Hornbækhus** 'The Block'
66	**Building Study 2: Vestersøhus** 'The Terrace'
88	**Building Study 3: Dronningegården** 'The Square'
116	**The Moral of Functionalism** *Kay Fisker*
124	**Response 1: Between Familiarity and Abstraction** Fisker in the Present Time *Tony Fretton*
126	**Response 2: Two Tone** *Job Floris*
129	**Response 3: Conversation and the Contingent** *Andrew Clancy and Colm Moore*
132	**Author Biographies**

Between Strategy and Detail:
Kay Fisker and the Conditions of Life

Andrew Clancy and Colm Moore

> 'A building should be a shell around the life to be lived within it, a shell that will satisfy material as well as intellectual demands. The architect creates not life, but conditions of life. Raymond Unwin once said: "We cannot create life, but we can form the channels of life in such a way that the sources of life will flow into them of their own accord."'
>
> *Kay Fisker*, 'The Moral of Functionalism', 1947

This book explores the work of the Danish architect Kay Otto Fisker, with reference to three housing projects in Copenhagen: Hornbækhus (1920–22), Vestersøhus (1935 and 1939), designed with C.F. Møller, and Dronningegården (1958), also designed with C.F. Møller and Svenn Eske Kristensen. Each represents an evolving thesis: a functional architecture founded on the conditions of life. Hornbækhus is the most widely known and celebrated of the three. This monumental block, measuring 200m by 80m, and comprising 290 apartments around a vast internal garden, proved to be a key moment in the evolution of Danish social housing and of the city of Copenhagen, with the birth of what became called the 'kilometre style'.

With both its scale and its economy of means, the building opened new horizons in the scale and nature of the housing projects that were to follow over the following half-century by Fisker and other Danish architects. This is not a book about theory, or history, although both are contained within it. More simply it is a documenting of three housing projects in detail so that the latent knowledge inherent in their fabric can be better read, understood and appreciated.

The same year that Hornbækhus was commissioned (1922), Le Corbusier published his plans for the Ville Contemporaine – a utopian community based around the avoidance of friction, and with functional efficiency as its maxim. Fisker's polemic is not written in words but in the building itself; its architecture establishes an infrastructure of encounter. It builds itself from a humane consideration of neighbourliness, and from the contingencies of available materials and skills.

Size does not have to preclude nuance. The large scale of this project, and the tuning of the elevation and its relief, offers the potential for something more. Nuance writ large offers a space for a gentle civic expression. We are drawn to Fisker's work for its demonstration of how to deploy the skills of an architect – not as a radical disruption, but as a negotiation of found conditions and the weaving into something that shapes the city.

Only six drawings of Hornbækhus survive: a plan, bursting at the margins of the page; two meticulously drawn elevations; and three sheets composed of window and door details at various scales. These six sheets describe the making of a city as a conversation between strategy and detail, their economy and precision describing the minimum required to enable habitation. The Hornbækhus makes for generous architecture using minimal means. It is an architecture of infrastructure. The extended line of its facade marks a territory within which a community has been graciously drawn together. Its deceptive simplicity belies the deep work and calibration applied to every aspect of its making.

This attitude lies most potently in the treatment of the building's facades. Although the structure is massive, its external facades are gentle, with windows expressed forward, facing the city, and accompanied by generous bands of plaster. These catch the light and dematerialise the large brick walls, the facade becoming a drawn curtain joined at each of its sharp corners by seams of plaster quoins. It is hung from a cornice, emphasising its character as a taut fabric addressing the city. It is possible to see this simultaneously in two ways: that the individual dwellings are completely subsumed into the urban gesture, only

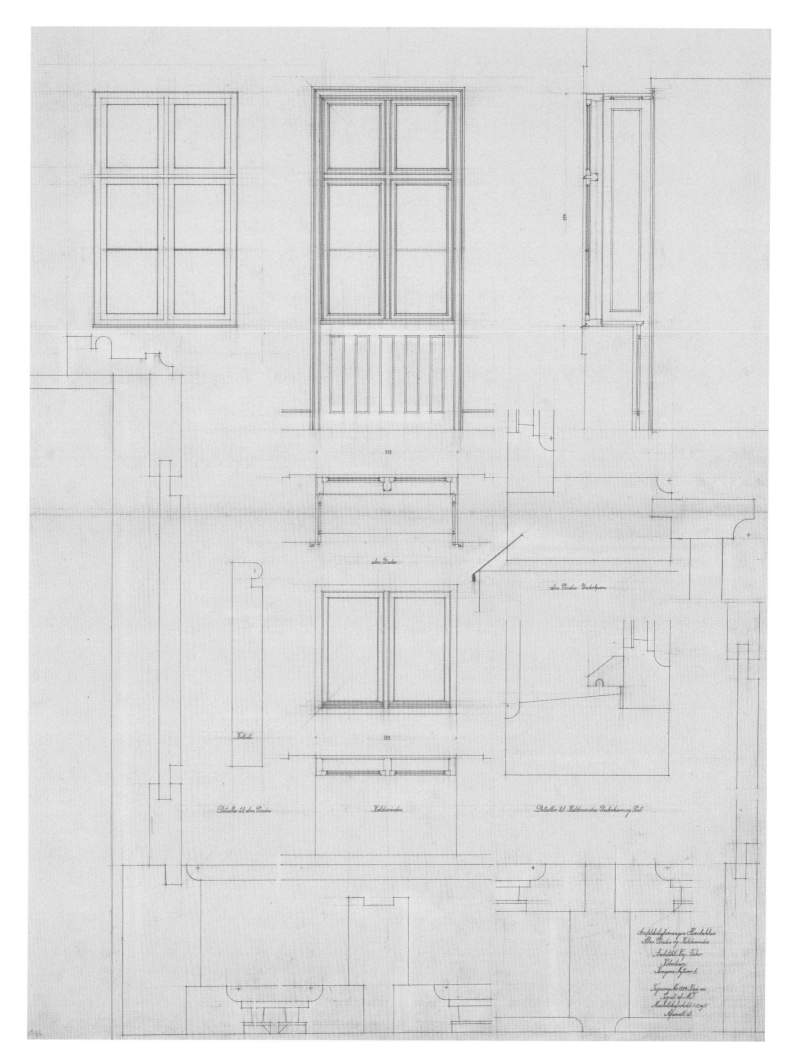

Windows in detail, Hornbækhus. Drawing from Kay Fisker Studio, 1920. The Danish National Art Library.

the doors, stretched tall, marking it as a house; and, conversely, as a facade made of windows, each calibrated to the individual, to life. The wall is a subsidiary matrix, a means of holding this society in collective form.

This same care is found in the stairs and entrances – tightly wound but offering each apartment a front and back door. The service stairs that gives access to the vast interior garden show more daily use than the more formal stairs addressing the street. Comings and goings, fronts and backs, privacy, gregariousness and a community all arrive in this simple gesture.

In contrast to the external facade, the internal face is defined by windows that are gently recessed, with no plastered surrounds. A stronger face is made to the more intimate enclosure; the internal corners of this communal room are chamfered to make its embrace complete. This careful articulation in relief presents a reposed external character in profile to the city, and an internal profile that establishes the strength of this building's community.

Fisker's working method has been documented by many who worked or studied with him. Poul Kjærgaard has written of Fisker's love of drawing, and his concern, not with the technology of construction, but with what he called 'the big lines' – the order and proportion of works. Find Moines describes how Fisker kept a private office, removed from but accessed through the practice's drafting room. Conversations about projects would take place privately, accompanied by light sketches in a notebook. Moines remarks that Fisker would engage with a project first by speaking about it, to define a strategy, and only after that would drawing begin.

Responding to the drawings, removed from the drafting room, Fisker acted as a negotiator, achieving the final architectural design through iterative adjustment of elements: the placement of a window, the height of a balcony, the location of the stairs.

The six drawings are emblematic of this method. Not chance survivors, they are in fact an accurate capturing of the contribution to architectural knowledge represented by Fisker's working method. They are a deliberate attempt to represent everything. They speak of the importance of the whole, of the relationship of archetype to typology. The drawings describe Fisker's architectural language, both in terms of style and ethics. We use the term 'architectural language' here in the shadow of Antonio Monestiroli's description of 'a formal system which accounts for the sense of buildings, and contains a general point of view on architecture. This language includes the technical laws of construction, the evocation of worlds of form, natural or historical; and identify, the unity of knowledge and representation.'

Fisker situated his work in the functionalist tradition, but with a caveat that he believed that regionalist requirements should be a fundamental part of functionalism, predating critical regionalism by over four decades. Fisker was building on the teaching and instruction of Peder Vilhelm Jensen-Klimt in his appreciation of the sculptural forms of large volumes and the textual value of materials, as a way to engage with vernacular architecture in the making of contemporary work. He repeatedly stressed the programmatic value of functionalist thinking – that it was more important than technology, tectonics or innovation in form.

If, in Fisker's definition, the question of material and form is grounded in Klimt's call for continuity as a key duty of functionalism, this raises the question of what then was Fisker's notion of programme? It is clear in examining his various projects that he was not interested in a radical reordering of the nature of dwelling via the plan of the individual unit. In his 1947 essay 'The Moral of Functionalism', Fisker defines programme as being 'the conditions of life' – something broader than an understanding of a dwelling unit, but opening a view that encompasses the city, the territory and the local collective spaces of the building. It is in this context that we can begin to understand Fisker's repeated, obsessive return to threshold spaces in relation to the whole.

Patrick Healy, in considering Monestiroli, traces the traditional connection between architecture and nature via mimesis, and this transmutation into an ever more detailed study of geometries and proportions – an approach that remains. We can see how Fisker's contemporaries engaged with this tradition. For Le Corbusier it was via a re-engagement with nature, in the form of industrial vernacular architecture on an elemental level. For Mies van der Rohe it was the tectonic, the potentials of the column, the window. For Loos it was through history. By foregrounding 'the conditions of life', Fisker grapples with the fundamental ethical imperative behind an architectural language – and indeed the potential for an ethical aesthetic. His architectural language represents a marrying of regional tradition and a creation of a civic form in which the individual and the collective are set in a finely balanced equilibrium.

In the potential for a style to be invented in the search for a language, there is a risk that these fundamental connections be lost in a self-referential engagement with the language itself, un-interrogated. In the case of Mies and Corbusier, in particular, this aspect is well understood, applied internationally without an investigation of local realities. In Fisker's architecture, style in this guise is less the issue, sited as it is in his understanding of regionalist traditions of making and inhabitation. Ideas walked their way from his buildings across housing projects in Copenhagen and elsewhere in Denmark but not much further. His ideas for gardens, doorways, balconies and windows appear in other architects' work with a precocious vitality. His impact was felt beyond his works, not by thinning out the ideas but in generously enabling others.

Today, architects literally draw everything. The proliferation of new drafting tools has enabled us to capture the world in its entirety. The ability to do so has quickly supplanted traditional architectural processes and means of representation, the drawing projection increasingly subsumed into more immediate multi-authored three-dimensional building information models: a profound development that we are still only coming to terms with in practice. It is obvious that these new digital processes require a different engagement. But in Fisker's work we find a reminder that before we can draw anything we need to be able to see clearly. He offers profound lessons on how a humane architecture can be made, one which can face the shared challenges of our time, while keeping in sight each individual inhabitant.

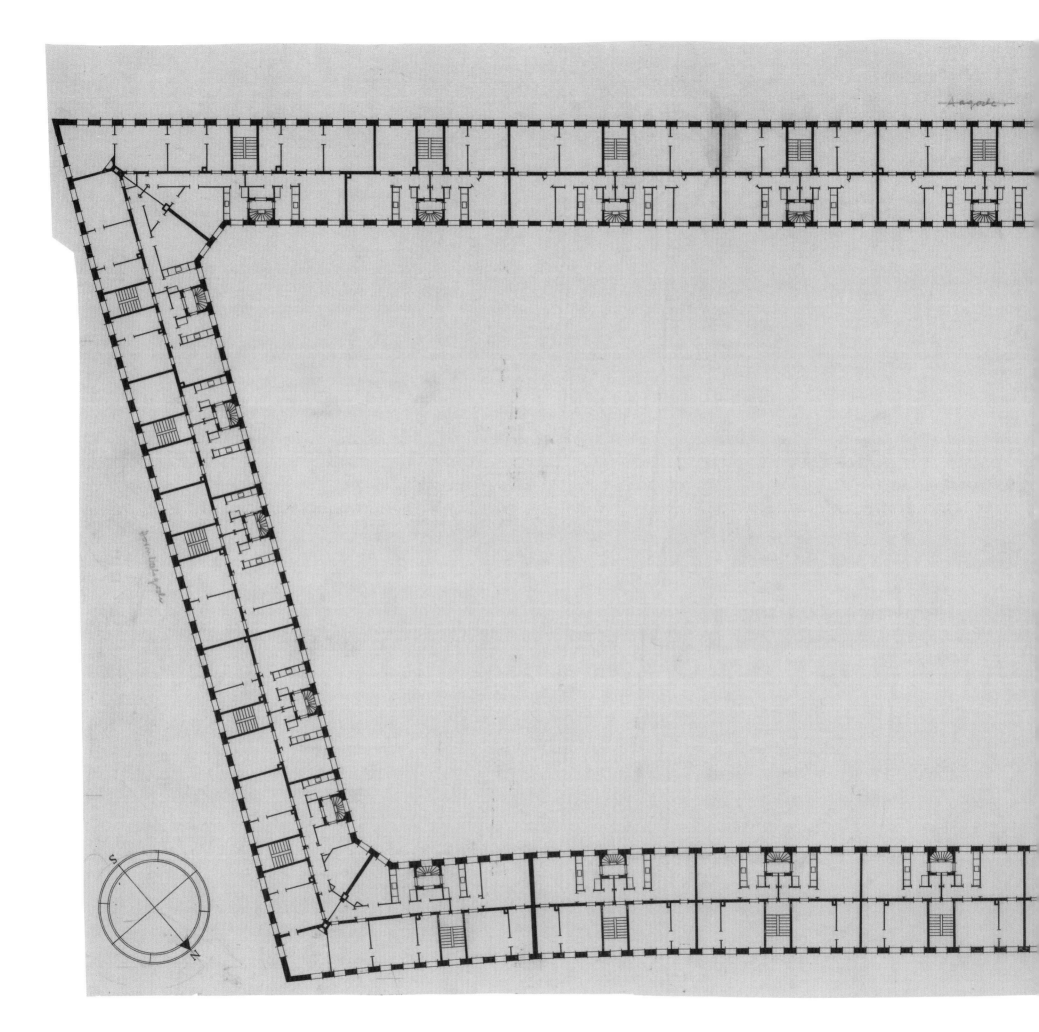

Typical floor, Hornbækhus. Drawing from Kay Fisker Studio, 1920. The Danish National Art Library.

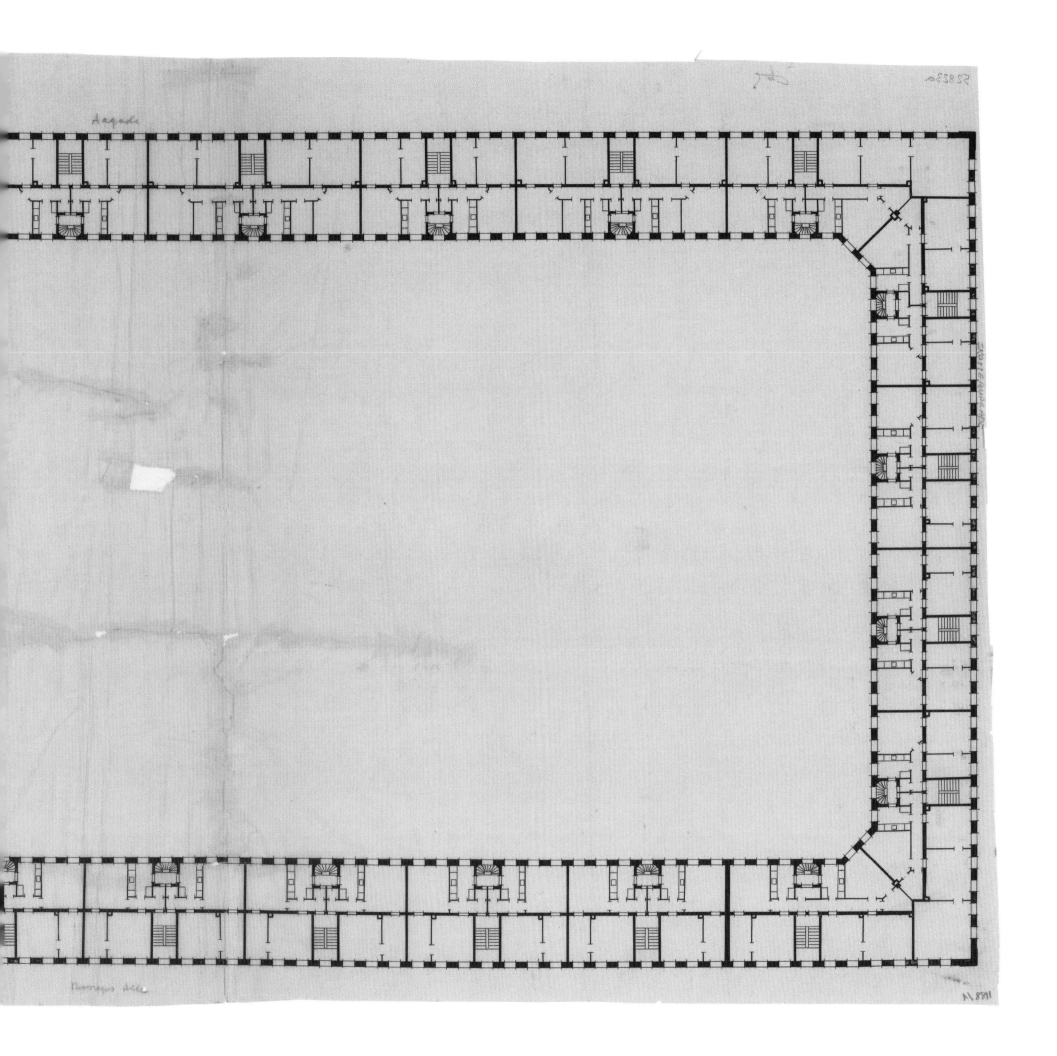

Facade mod Borups allé.

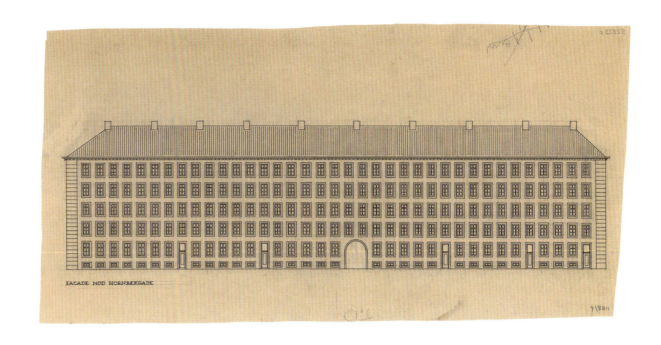

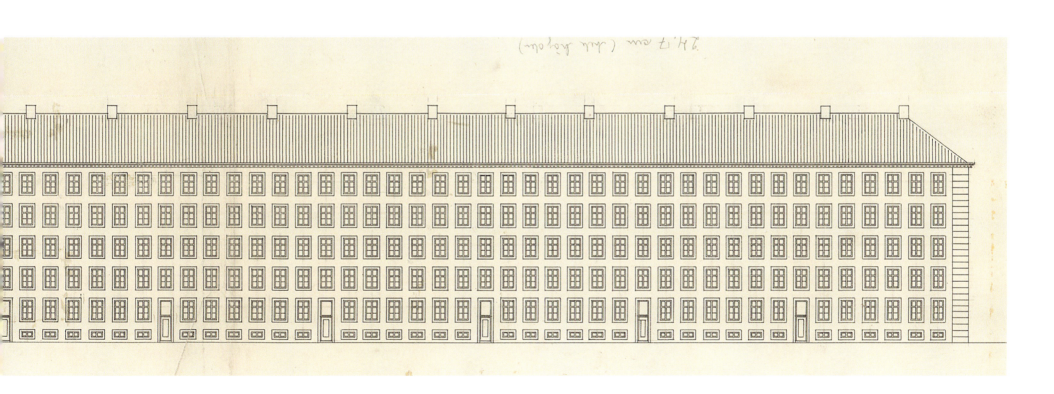

Above: short elevation of Hornbækhus on to Hornbækgade.
Below: long elevation of Hornbækhus on to Borups Allé.
The Danish National Art Library.

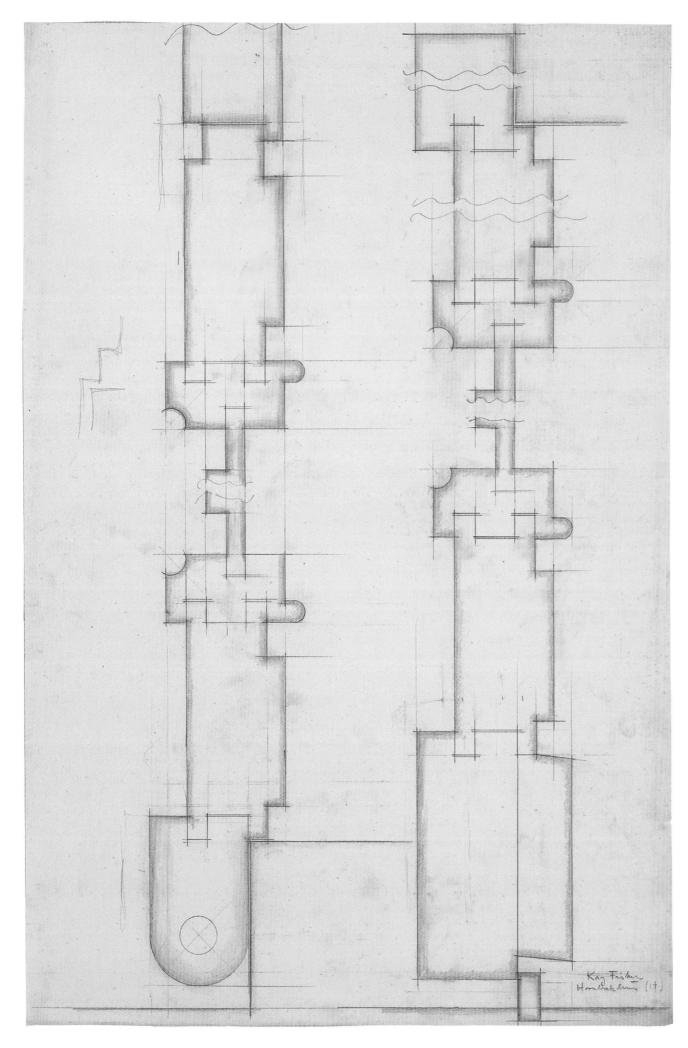

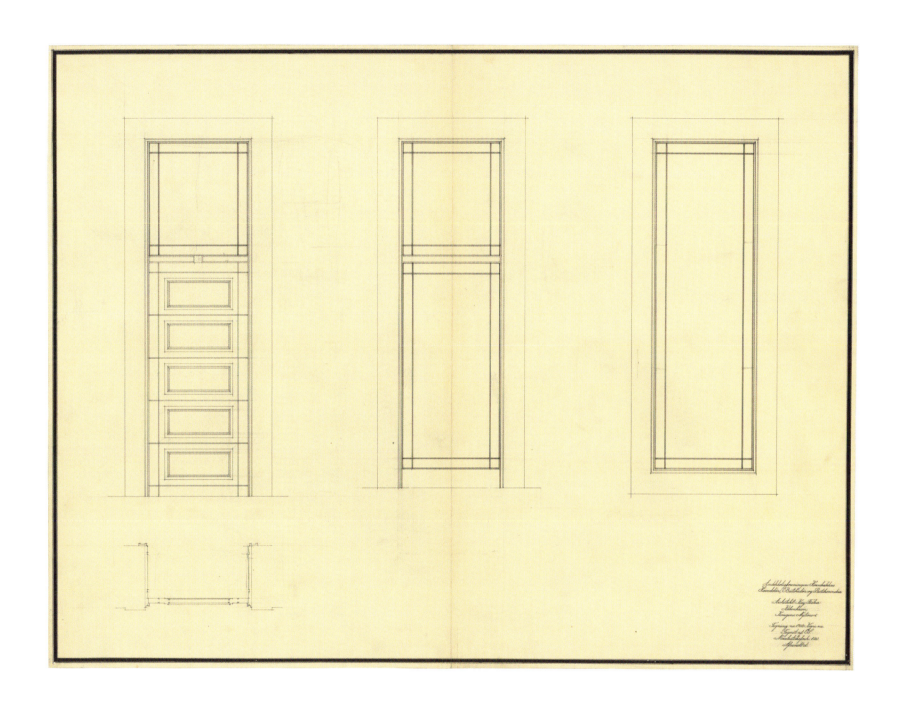

Opposite: front door sections, Hornbækhus. Above: front door elevation and window drawing set, Hornbækhus. Drawings from Kay Fisker Studio, 1920. The Danish National Art Library.

Kay Fisker's Classical Principles for Modern Housing

Martin Søberg

Societal changes were a substantial influence on Danish architecture during the first decades of the 20th century. The regulation of rent levels was intended to secure the situation of people renting flats – to further diminish the consequences of the housing crisis, and to promote the construction of more housing. A law was passed in 1917 aimed at financially supporting the housing construction industry. Between 1922 and 1927, this was further supported by Statsboligfonden (State Housing Foundation). In Copenhagen, many of the large housing schemes built during the 1920s were a direct consequence of these initiatives, further supported by the fact that the municipality of Copenhagen frequently functioned as a commissioner of housing projects.

With land prices kept down by the municipality, which owned major plots of land, new typological possibilities for the design of mass housing arose. One of the first of these rather large projects was Povl Baumann's perimeter block, built for the municipality in the working-class district of Nørrebro around Struenseegade in 1919–20. Yet, even prior to that and before the War, in 1912, Charles J. Schou had designed housing schemes in the Nørrebro and Sønderbro districts in which buildings framed a common courtyard with little or no protrusion of the block into the yard, as had been typical hitherto in the privately commissioned projects constructed around the turn of the century (and often motivated by financial speculation).

In 1936, Kay Fisker published the results of research into Copenhagen housing typologies, covering the period from 1914 to 1936. The most obvious change during this period, according to Fisker, was the transition from traditional perimeter blocks – which had dominated the Copenhagen cityscape for centuries – to new types of distribution, mainly constructed during the 1930s, including half-closed schemes, parallel houses, projects consisting of composition of blocks, or houses positioned at a 90-degree angle.

The influence of these studies of changing housing typologies can be seen in Fisker's own mass housing projects in Copenhagen during the 1920s and 1930s. Hornbækhus (1920–22) is particularly significant, both in terms of scale and typology. The project leaves the centre of the perimeter block completely open as a collective green space, complete with large flowerbeds. It was a scheme which Fisker would develop further in Jagtgaarden (1924) with Christian Holst and Gullfosshus (1927). The perimeter is retained in these projects, and they all feature classical elements such as a symmetrical arrangement of the facades, cornices and tripartitions. But rather than stylistic imitations, the architectural theory supporting these projects was founded on objectivity and rationalisation. Fisker's relationship with classicism was not directed towards an exact imitation of a particular historical style; his attitude was not archaeological. It leaned towards certain classical architectural principles to resonate with modern conceptions of what a contemporary city could be. Rather than recreating the past, it was a question of learning from the past in order to direct and construct the future.

Fisker supported the rational classicism of his contemporaries. Carl Petersen and Ivar Bentsen's competition project for the Copenhagen railway terrain from 1919 demonstrated the expressive power of restricted form. Even before the competition, Bentsen

Kay Fisker, competition project for a nursing home, Frederiksberg, 1919. The Danish National Art Library.

had published a proposal for this area, an opera and philharmonic building that included offices and a shop, with repetitive bays and windows sized according to the golden section. Then editor of Danish magazine *Architekten*, Fisker supported the quest for new typologies and rational principles. In a review in the journal *Forskønnelsen* of the Danish translation of the Swedish art historian Gregor Paulsson's book *Den nya arkitekturen* (1916), Fisker wrote: 'Principally speaking, where he [Paulsson] works for a suppression of individualism, for an objective art, uniform architecture, typification and standardisation of the forms, he stands out as strong and true and in touch with his time.'[1] The review was illustrated with the perspective and plan of Carl Petersen and Ivar Bentsen's competition project for the Copenhagen railway terrain, by which Fisker indicated exactly what sort of architecture he would consider to be 'in touch with his time': objective and uniform architecture.

The restricted, repetitive architectural language and large-scale typologies of Bentsen's and Petersen's railway terrain projects resonate with Fisker's projects from the same period – the end of the 1910s – such as the 1918 first prize competition scheme for a housing block at Store Vibenshus in Copenhagen. It featured a concave facade adjusting to the shape of a large circular piazza, tall windows with French balconies, rusticated corners and a massive cornice crowned by a balustrade hiding the roof. The competition was arranged by the municipality, but the project was never realised. Hans Erling Langkilde describes these early urban projects in his 1960 monograph on Fisker as follows: 'There is something cleansed and utterly completed about his houses – an independent tone that makes superflous the familiar qualities which usually belong to this period of time. After all, the Vibenhus project is more dependent on the spirit of classicism than on its props.'[2]

Though the functional programme is different, Fisker's attempt to use geometry and rational principles as a guideline to achieve a sense of order was developed to an even higher degree in his project for a racing track on the island of Amager, on the outskirts of Copenhagen in 1919–22. It was developed into a final tender stage, but disagreements between Fisker and the commissioner concerning payments resulted in Fisker being dismissed. The Amager Racing Track would comprise a variety of spaces from the compartmentalisation of the horse stables to the vast collective spaces of restaurants, lobbies and viewing platforms. It was clearly conceived as a modern recreational facility, situated close to a tram station and to the proposed Copenhagen airport, which, however, would not open until years later. Various perspective drawings show a rhythmic grouping of cubic volumes and the entire complex is surrounded by trees as a sort of framework. The buildings form a classical pavilion system, with several square parts in different heights and sizes, framing several courtyards.

A drawing of the Amager project in a bird's-eye perspective illustrates the new and very urban sense of scale that was also to be found in contemporary projects such as those of Bentsen and Petersen, in Fisker's Hornbækhus, and, later, in his Jagtgaarden and Gullfosshus projects, amongst others. The large open room was activated by the movement during the races, framed by plants like a wall, while buildings along one of the longer sides consisted of a continuous pavilion system, mostly one-storey high, surrounding six square courtyards, some of which were attached to an even bigger courtyard.

Examining some of the plans for this project, it becomes clear that the square is a generating entity, forming a grid as a basis for the layout of the entire building scheme. This simple shape spreads across the ground and constitutes the full complex, binding together horses and people. Concurrently, the building contains a certain hierarchy, partly due to the tripartition with restaurant and tribunes placed in the middle on two floors, while the stables seem to subordinate to this core entity. The stables themselves are of particular interest, since they mainly consist of square horse boxes, connected with hallways. That is, a system of individual cells connected to an infrastructure, itself being linked with the major public space: the restaurant. The entire complex thereby forms a sort of mini version of an urban situation, a community in which the housing of the horses is literally put into boxes yet joined to a monumental centre, the open landscape, and the actual infrastructure of the racing track.

Apart from the many other differences, one also finds an ensemble of individual cells – the flats, the surrounding infrastructure and the open landscape in the courtyard of the Hornbækhus housing project. We might consider Fisker to be working with a total structure in various projects, and though the plan of Hornbækhus is much more varied, the Amager Racing Track, along with his early competition projects, is an investigation into the formation of contemporary and later projects, as well as some of their urban principles. That being said, the plan layout of

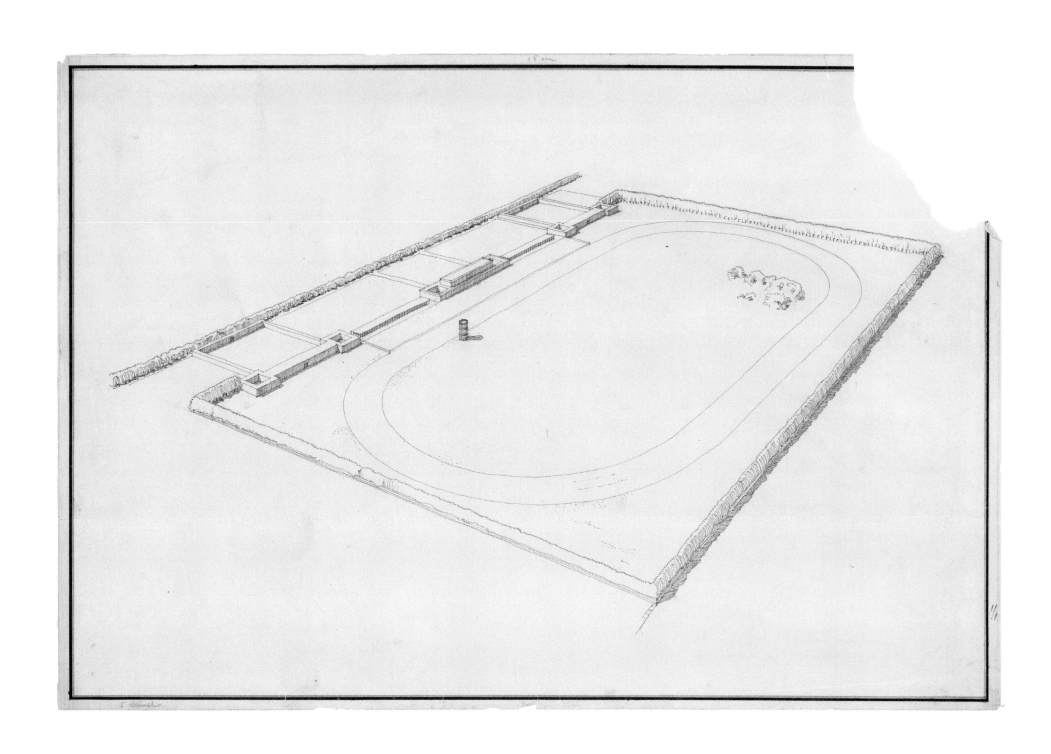

Kay Fisker, Amager Racing Track, 1919–22. The Danish National Art Library.

Hornbækhus is also an adjusted figure and thereby very different from the pure geometries of the racing track. Its rectangular form slightly adjusts to the curvature of the street at Borups Allé, while a similar curvature is absent along the street of Ågade, where the longest of the four facades stretches as a full plane as if to emphasise the almost endless repetition of facade elements, such as windows – yet this horizontal recurrence is contracted by the rusticated corners.

If the facade features repetition, then the plan is in fact revealed to be more complex, for the building contains a significant number of different plan solutions, determined by their position within the perimeter. The corners, in particular, contribute to this differentiation.[3] As Fisker would state in a lecture given in Helsinki in 1927: '… the highest virtues of architecture are to be found in proportions, demanding meticulous consideration of every aspect. […] The material is no longer judged for its fineness or historical justification but for its relation to its surroundings, colour and surface treatment, which in itself is also a proportionality consideration.'[4]

Steen Eiler Rasmussen, architect and teacher at the Royal Danish Academy's School of Architecture, like Fisker, stated: 'The enormous size of the house is shown by means of the hundreds of windows of equal sizes, windows which their grey frames bind together in long horizontal lines. The architect has emphasised the main features: dimensions and space … He finds an almost pedantic order, and uniformity essential in such buildings; and that is quite logical. The subject is a collection of equal elements.'[5] But even if the dimensions would seem to contradict the existing scale of the city, we might as well consider it an attempt to adjust to a new vision of urbanity. This is a building that adheres to the modern city of mass population and unforeseen speed – the speed of cars, aeroplanes or even racing horses. In this sense, it is proportionate to the requirements of a contemporary metropolis.

Kay Fisker considered modern architecture as a pursuit of an ultimate solution and form. Yet such a pursuit would not require the architect to establish a sort of avant-garde attitude, the presentation of the hitherto unseen and utterly original. It was rather an attempt to consider and develop existing models within the typologies and registers of housing. In what has been termed Fisker's architectural testament, the essay 'Persondyrkelse eller anonymitet' ('Cult of Personality or Anonymity'), published in 1964, he points to the architect's obligation to subordinate themselves and their artistic will to the needs of human beings rather than attempting to create the spectacular: 'We must remember that those architects who order our cityscapes and our landscape, and who manage to create a human environment with decent housing as the setting for a good way of life, are worth more to society than those who create individual and sensational works of art.'[6] Though this essay was written decades after the design and construction of the estates of the 1920s, a similar poetic stance seems to have been at work then: architecture considered a built framework for the daily life of people, whilst concurrently forming part of a total cityscape.

NOTES
1. Kay Fisker, 'Architekturbetragtninger', *Forskønnelsen* 1 (1921), pp 1–4.
2. Hans Erling Langkilde, *Arkitekten Kay Fisker*, Copenhagen: Arkitektens Forlag, 1960, p.24.
3. Stephen Bates, Bruno Krucker, and Katharina Leuschner, eds., *Hornbækhus Building Register*, Munich: TU München, 2013.
4. Fisker, quoted in Kirmo Mikkola, 'The Transition from Classicism to Functionalism in Scandinavia', in *Classical Tradition and the Modern Movement,* ed. Asko Salokorpi, Helsinki: Finnish Association of Architects, 1985, pp 42–73.
5. Steen Eiler Rasmussen, 'A Modern Danish Architect: Kay Fisker', *The Architect & Building News*, 3 February, 1928, pp 189–92.
6. Kay Fisker, 'Persondyrkelse eller anonymitet', *Arkitekten* 66, no. 26, 1964, pp 522–6.

Main garden, Hornbækhus.

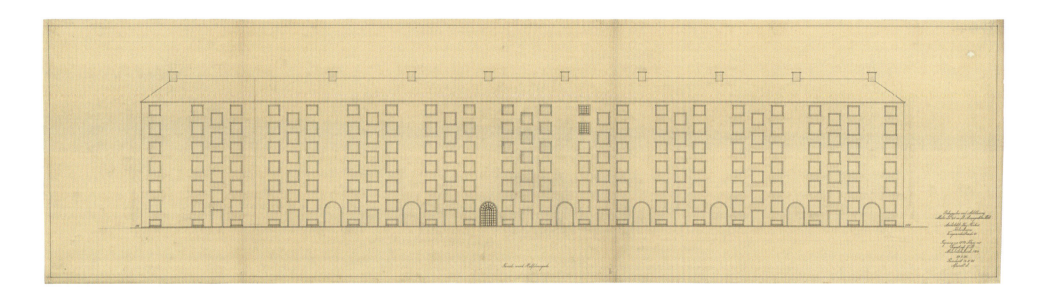

Gulfosshus: elevation to Gullfossgade. Kay Fisker 1924–7.
The Danish National Art Library..

Kay Fisker, Gulfosshus, 1924–7. The Danish National Art Library.

Gulfosshus central garden.

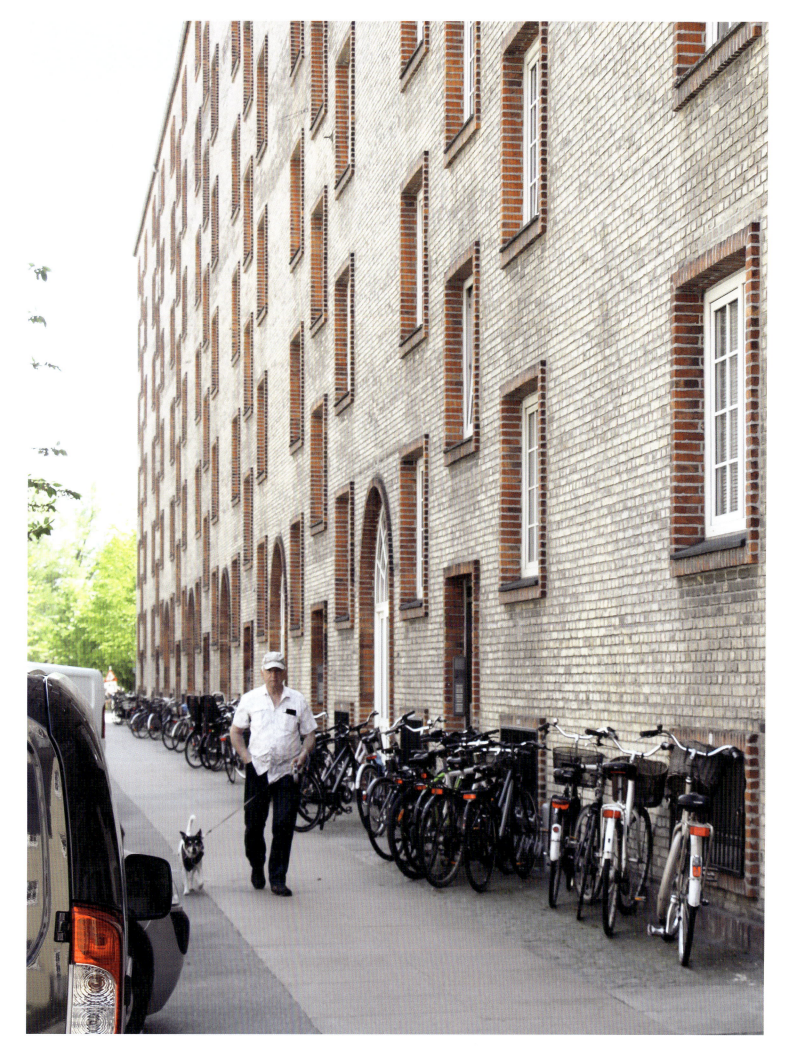
Gulfosshus: facade to Halfdansgade.

An Outline of Danish Social Housing History

Poul Sverrild

The emerging industrialisation at the midpoint of the 19th century created a new class of workers previously unseen in Danish society. This rapidly growing group of underprivileged citizens were deprived of the fundamental rights that had hitherto followed employment in the traditional trades, where the employer was responsible for wages alongside housing and food. This led to a radical change in the established household structure creating a large number of small, economically unstable households living in tenements with little fresh air, poor water supply and inadequate sanitation.

This phenomenon, combined with an explosive growth of the population within the fortification of the city, due to a ban on development outside of the city walls, led to a chronic shortage of housing in Copenhagen. It was with the outbreak of a severe cholera epidemic in 1853 that the housing situation became acutely problematic. This resulted in the construction of several housing developments built by philanthropic organisations, the first example of which was the development known as Brumleby (1857) in Østerbro, commissioned by the Danish Medical Society, with the first phase of construction designed by the architect Michael Gottlieb Bindesbøll. This scheme is considered Denmark's first example of social housing.

This philanthropical response evolved throughout the 1860s. Housing organisations, such as the Danish Medical Society, sought to enable the collective purchase of land by groups of workers, and the development of these sites to provide housing – each of which would then be owned by an individual worker and their family. A subtext here was the aspiration that promoting home ownership would aid in the establishment of a conservative political class. In the 1890s, the first national legislation was passed providing cheap building loans to associations of workers. The aim was individual ownership – with the model being individual small houses on their own lands that were to become the predominant typology of private dwellings in Denmark for at least the next century.

A new kind of association started to appear just before World War I. Workers organised themselves into collectives, with the aim being to provide dwellings on a rental basis. The ownership of the buildings would remain collective, as would the ongoing management and maintenance, once completed. The individual temptations arising from speculative profit would be avoided. This system, with privately organised non-profit housing associations providing dwellings, was how 'social housing' came to be organised in Denmark. Municipal or government-owned housing never came to play a role. In principle, the sector provided housing for anyone, not only the poorer sections of society. For over 80 years, until the late 1960s, this secured a very broad social basis for the recruitment of tenants and prevented a marked profile as 'social housing' being different or more problematic than other forms of housing.

The non-profit housing associations grew from a very modest start between the world wars to become the dominant factor behind shaping the new city. The strong ideologies informing these organisations placed an emphasis on experimentation with a view to developing robust, humane and socially cohesive designs.

Helped by prominent architects, the associations developed new architectural forms and set new standards for dwellings measured by size, installations and access to healthy surroundings. After World War II, the scale of the housing problem became once again severe. In recognition of this, the associations, working in partnership with the government, sought to lead the reform of the building industry. The projects changed from small scale to grand plan, from brick to concrete, on-site to prefab and from skilled to unskilled workers. All this took place in the new suburbs.

The associations raised the quality of living tremendously, aiming to provide the average family with a room for each member of the family. In addition, they supplied the projects with open space, healthy green areas, integrated shopping facilities, kindergartens, and so on. This took place within the framework of the overall planning agenda driven by local government. The housing shortage was practically extinct by the early 1970s and the housing standards were unparalleled.

The glorious epoch of seemingly endless growth for the associations ended with the realisation of the big scale residential plans of the 1970s. Criticisms of the consequences of the industrialisation of the housing sector had been audible from around 1970, but the political and economic interests in the sector were such that it took nearly a decade for the problems to be recognised. Globalisation was leading to a dwindling number of industrial workplaces and the combination of unemployment and immigration were not easy to address within the collective housing model.

In addition, the fabric of some of the estates was threatened by crumbling concrete – the pace to innovate had outstripped the ability to build well. All of these forces were compounded by the high interest rates on loans that were a feature of the late 1970s and early 1980s.

Since then the conversation in modernist suburbia and social housing projects in Denmark has been dominated by the seemingly endless problems caused by social segregation, materiality, economy and aesthetics. This has for long overshadowed the fact that the government, the associations, the architects and the entrepreneurs actually did the job everybody wanted done: abolishment of the housing shortage. We are actually talking about a success here. The creation of the physical framework of the welfare state. And all the goals that were formulated at the starting point were accomplished. The world changed along the way but this remains an abiding achievement.

Dronningegården and Kay Fisker's Continuum

Job Floris

During the post-war reconstruction years modernism appears to have dominated the Dutch architecture discourse, thereby effectively marginalising all other developments and perspectives. Kay Fisker can be seen as one of the few critical voices, which is why he remains a relatively unknown figure within the Dutch context. This is unfortunate, because there is a lot of common ground between Fisker's agenda and both the Dutch and wider European discourses. In 1948 he garnered attention in the Netherlands with 'Louis Henry Sullivan', an article about the architect's life and work, published in leading journal *Forum*.[1] The article is a testament to Fisker's strong belief in continuity, putting modernism into perspective and identifying precedents.

In the article, Fisker focused on the period of irrepressible urbanisation in Chicago and the tradition of metropolitan architecture in general, topics that reflected issues from his own practice. Fisker made a thorough study of Louis H. Sullivan (1856–1924), as suggested by the detailed descriptions of the American's architectural interests, career and personal life. This was not entirely new: at the time Sullivan's influence could be seen in the Netherlands in the work of Hendrik Petrus Berlage. A meeting with Sullivan in 1893 had had a profound effect on the Dutch architect's oeuvre. Above all, Fisker proved himself a critical admirer of Sullivan's work, recognising shared interests and describing his realised buildings as 'peculiarly individualistic' and very much a product of their time. Fisker's interest in Sullivan seems to have been prompted by the latter's pioneering role in the transition from an academic Beaux-Arts tradition to 'new directions' in architecture.

Fisker assumed that the modern movement's adoption of Sullivan's credo, 'form follows function', must have been unacceptable to the American architect because of its narrow interpretation. Fisker must have seen Sullivan as a kindred spirit, since he occupied a similarly ambivalent position, having abandoned the classical vocabulary while at the same time displaying a critical attitude towards modernism. This attitude appears to have been inspired by both Sullivan himself and his student Frank Lloyd Wright (1867–1959), as suggested by the article in which Fisker quotes from the Kahn Lectures in 1930, in which Wright speaks against the Machine Aesthetic:

> 'A home is a machine to live in, a chair is a machine to sit in and the human body is a machine to be worked by mind. A tree is a machine to bear fruit, a plant is a machine to bear flowers and seeds, and a heart is a pump. Does that thrill you? The least any of these things only may be is just that.'[2]

The platform for publication of Fisker's article was selected with care. At the time, *Forum* sought to bring about a dialogue between the modernists and traditionalists. The article made it clear that Fisker was looking for kindred spirits, both old and new. Historian Stanford Anderson categorises Fisker's work as 'New Empiricism'[3] and places him in a European discourse with kindred spirits in Great Britain and Switzerland. Fisker himself labelled his approach as 'Functional Traditionalism'.[4]

The article on Sullivan fits into a wider context. Fisker studied a number of architects with a similar approach, even though he did not state this explicitly. He identifies

The alternating pattern of the court facade. Photo: Job Floris.

precedents, stressing the fact that Sullivan was taught by Henry Hobson Richardson (1838–86) and that their work did not receive due recognition until the success of Sullivan's student Wright. Among those Fisker studied were the British architects C.F.A. Voysey (1857–1941), Mackay Hugh Baillie-Scott (1865–1945) and German architect Heinrich Tessenow (1876–1950). Fisker generously shared his enthusiasm for their work in both his articles and lectures.

Historian Lisbet Balslev Jorgensen outlines how, around 1920, Tessenow was a particularly significant reference point in the Danish discourse.[5] One of the key voices in this debate was that of Danish architect Peder Vilhelm Jensen-Klint (1853–1930). The authority argued for architecture with more homogeneity, reflecting regional elements and showing evidence of a thoughtful approach to materiality. The work of German architects such as Peter Behrens (1868–1940) was followed closely in Denmark and seen as an overly bombastic alternative to classicism. Tessenow's work formed a welcome exception to this trend. His book *Hausbau und dergleichen* ('House building and such', 1916) was thought to set the right tone for architecture in Denmark.[6] His architecture stood for craftsmanship, combined with a degree of austerity and cohesion that was clearly based on classical conventions. These aspects were adhered to by the Danish architectural community and also formed the leitmotif in the work of Fisker, who clearly viewed the architectural field as a continuum of precedents. Fisker put modernism into perspective by focusing on the human scale and on haptic perception, which came to be an intrinsic part of his architecture.

Making the city

From 1920 Fisker realised an impressive series of colossal metropolitan apartment blocks in Copenhagen, among them Hornbækhus (1920–22) and buildings on Englandsvej (1924–6), Vognmandsmarken (1925–7), Artillerivej (1927), Vodroffsvej (1932), Fogedgården (1943–5) and the Dronningegården complex (1943–58). Fisker had a studio in Copenhagen and worked on housing commissions in different partnerships. Many of his designs came about in collaboration with C.F. Møller (1898–1988), including Dronningegården, which was a joint design with Møller and Svenn Eske Kristensen (1905–2000). When viewed chronologically it becomes clear that the designs are all variations on one and the same theme. The result is a series of surprisingly sober and lean city blocks of an immense size. Fisker introduces a layering to these projects that imbues them with both large-scale monumentality and small-scale intimacy. Nearly all of his housing complexes feature a strict repetition of window openings, set in stripped-down, austere facades. This basic rhythm creates calm and cohesion and seems to stress the width and height of the building mass as a whole. This results in near 'infinity', as the individual dwelling is completely subordinated to the urban gesture. However, sober accents make the abstract blocks more approachable and accessible as a housing block. When viewed up close the initial rigidity of the blocks is softened by small protrusions and frames that draw attention to the collective entrances.

All of the housing complexes are made of the same basic material, with the brick bond patterns providing the necessary intricacy. Fisker must have decided to respond to new challenges in large-scale housing by starting with and then developing conventional, local techniques and materials. Many of the residential complexes are characterised by a simple but effective section, which is extruded as it were and situated efficiently alongside the plot perimeter. With this narrow, tall section Fisker establishes a clear distinction between the formal exterior and the informal interior formed by large, green collective courtyards. It makes Dronningegården considerably more complex and ambiguous than earlier housing blocks that all looked as if they were based on the same straightforward, solid and unambiguous template.

Dronningegården

The Dronningegården ensemble is situated just outside Copenhagen's historic city centre. The area is part of the partially realised expansion scheme known as 'New Copenhagen' (1650), which was meant to develop the fortified stronghold. The urban extension consists of a small grid, with the Dronningens Tværgade axis as the planned link between two public gardens: Kongens Have, a garden for King Frederick III (housing the current Rosenborg Castle) and a garden for Queen Sophie Amalia (where the former summer palace Sophie Amalienborg is located). In the end, the public garden for Queen Sophie Amalia was sacrificed for urban expansion, leaving the current Amalienborg square as a relic of the garden.

In 1943, building began on a new large-scale housing complex along this axis, to replace the dilapidated 17th-century buildings. This new ensemble, designed by Fisker

View from the court to Dronningens Tværgade. Photo: Job Floris.

in the shape of a large quadrangle, stresses the former axiality and subtly restores the connection between Kongens Have and Sophie Amalienborg. Fisker's new 'outdoor living room', which he had initially proposed as a green foyer to Kongens Have,[7] is typologically similar to Amalienborg square. In impressions, Fisker optimistically depicted the courtyard as a park. Its current use as a car park began early, however, and to this day the courtyard does not function as the green foyer he envisaged.

The new configuration that Fisker introduces to the small-scale urban fabric looks so big and autonomous at first sight that it appears to be creating new conditions. The complex features 72 apartments per floor and 20 vertical circulation points. The ground floor on Borgergade consists of commercial spaces topped by eight floors and some 620 apartments. However, on an intermediate scale, between urban design and architecture, the intervention is full of ambiguities that show that the complex was very carefully planned and complements the existing urban fabric. The monumental quadrangle is a collection of four masses, all of which are different because they respond to the diverse conditions of their surroundings. The demolished 17-century buildings were small in scale and the geometry of the new complex reflects this as the large configuration is reduced to a staccato rhythm of large houses lined up along Borgergade.

Fisker opted unequivocally for articulating the interior structure: the living quarters are all in the houses with the gable roofs, while the services cores are in the recessed corridors – a typically functionalist design technique. The first and last houses are set back, thus forming the quadrangle. Additionally, these parts of the block's interior are articulated like side walls, completely different from the end elevation.

The gable roof is an important means of expression, used here to accentuate the tall end elevations. Expressive roof forms are a tried and tested motif for Fisker, who applied them to the striking end elevations of the Mødrehjælpen office block and the University of Aarhus – although by then he had already used a flat roof with ribbon windows in the housing complex on Vodroffsvej from 1932. The repeated use of this motif shows that, despite the changing times, Fisker saw it as one of the fundamental elements of architecture. From this perspective, the use of conventional elements such as gable roofs becomes a polemic gesture, aimed above all at toning down a modern layout, showing that this convention deserves to be continued rather than abandoned.

Tactility and Materiality

As in the aforementioned housing blocks, the cohesion of Dronningegården can be attributed, first and foremost, to the fact that Fisker restricts himself to one basic material: yellow and red Danish brick. It is a pragmatic choice, as this regional product, unlike concrete, can be used without excessive transport costs or instruction. The building's entire basic volume consists of red brick. Fisker tackles all architectural problems within these material constraints and manages to find space for experimentation and detailing within this limited bandwidth. He successfully deploys the yellow brick to break the monumentality of the red building mass. He does so with yellow brick cross patterns as well as yellow brick frames that accentuate all perforations including the collective entrances and the low colonnade between Borgergade and the courtyard.

The project's most experimental dimension is its alternating facade pattern, created by the alternation between window opening and loggia. This intriguing intervention gives the building both an open and a massive countenance. The loggias are all 'lined' with yellow brick, resulting in an impressive sculptural look, which is particularly strong in a diagonal direction. Deep ridges compensate for the overly slender piers. Merely three headers wide, these look ill-equipped to fulfil their supporting function. The outer two yellow bricks have been turned out a quarter, while the red brick header in the middle continues the facade plane. This technique throws the convention into sharp relief. The facade looks like a cross between a massive classical surface in which the openings can be seen as perforations, surrounded by sufficient mass for the transfer of weight, and a constructed facade consisting of an arrangement of columns and beams. The resulting statement combines the extremes of a heavy, load-bearing mass and a filigree fabric. And yet Fisker remains consistent in his approach by treating the loggia as an excavation from the red brick mass, with a yellow brick lining or inlay that protrudes subtly out of the continuous red brick facade. Likewise, the seamless brickwork with set-back joints contributes to the material, textured character of the complex. The alternating facade pattern evokes the Grosvenor Estate, a London housing estate from 1930, designed by Sir Edwin Lutyens (1869-1944), which features a facade finish that, by and large, is not reflected in the floor plan. A substantial proportion of Kay Fisker's oeuvre consists of mass housing. He designed comfortable, affordable homes and always favoured the collective over the

View from Adelgade into the court. Photo: Job Floris.

individual. They are mainly sober buildings in the public sector rather than private mansions for the upper echelons of society. The power of large numbers enabled Fisker to build a city using big, clear configurations. And although these housing complexes offered only limited scope for experimentation, Fisker chose his means judiciously and achieved the best possible results. He took a pragmatic approach, always focusing on both craftsmanship and the reality of what was viable. The result is a series of related buildings that are remarkably striking, straightforward and efficient. Their detailing not withstanding, they remain bulky, severe and inelegant, the antithesis of the qualities usually attributed to Scandinavian classicist architecture.

Fisker's greatest quality as an architect was his analytical approach. That approach produced a dynamic balance between convention and new junctures. He was always questioning and developing instead of fixing and narrowing his vocabulary. In another text, 'The Moral of Functionalism' (1947),[8] Fisker argued that functionalism was presented as an extremely revolutionary, contemporary movement, while it effectively originated in the 19th century, and that the development of the associated vocabulary is all that is left. He also remarked that: 'The architecture of the past should be studied as the classical scholar studies Latin: not in order to speak the language but to understand its structure and coherence.'

NOTES
1. Prof. Kay Fisker, 'Louis Henry Sullivan', *Forum*, no.12 (November 1948), pp 347–55.
2. Ibid.
3. Stanford Anderson, 'The "New Empiricism: Bay Region Axis"', Kay Fisker and Postwar Debates on Functionalism, Regionalism and Monumentality', *Journal of Architectural Education*, vol. 50 (1984), no.3, pp 197–207.
4. Michael Asgaard Andersen, *Nordic Architects Write. A Documentary Anthology*, London: Routledge, 2008, pp 35-9.
5. Lisbet Balslev Jørgensen, in S. Paavilainen and J. Pallasmaa (eds.), *Nordic Classicism 1910–1930*, Helsinki: Museum of Finnish Architecture, 1982, exhibition catalogue, pp 51–6.
6. Ibid. Tessenow's book *Hausbau und dergleichen* was published in 1916 in Berlin by Bruno Cassirer.
7. 'Kay Fisker 1893-1965', special issue of *Archithese*, no.4, 1985, p.37.
8. Andersen, *Nordic Architects Write*, op. cit.

Door detail. Photo: Job Floris

Building Study 1: Hornbækhus
'The Block'

Hornbækhus, Copenhagen

Student researchers: Stephen McClelland, Mark Scott, Natalie Taylor, Darragh Tracey

Architects: Kay Fisker, Gudmund Nyeland Brandt, Poul Henningsen
Completed in 1923

Hornbækhus represents the beginning of Kay Fisker's career in social housing. Stretching almost 200m in length and 80m in width, comprised of 29 staircases, five floors and containing 290 apartments, the building follows the form of its block precisely. Bounded by Borups Allé, Hornbækgade, Skotterupgade and Ågade, the scheme forms a thin perimeter to a central green space. It provides one of the first modern examples of an architect and landscape architect collaborating on a social housing project.

Designed by Danish landscape architect Gudmund Nyeland Brandt, the courtyard acts as a focal point of the community, where residents share facilities such as playing courts, outdoor barbeques and washing lines.

Its scale is approaching that of a municipal park, providing a haven where the community of the building can gather, with families socialising and children playing in safety. The ground floor level is approximately 1.2m above street level, providing privacy to the lower apartments whilst also allowing light and ventilation to the basement below. The basement, with its individual storage spaces, is also accessed from the communal garden.

Living rooms face on to the street, kitchens and bedrooms face into the courtyard, to which the window stays consistent irrespective of its location or what is behind. Hornbækhus is a functional monument to repetition and simplicity, tuned to its inhabitants both as individuals and as a collective.

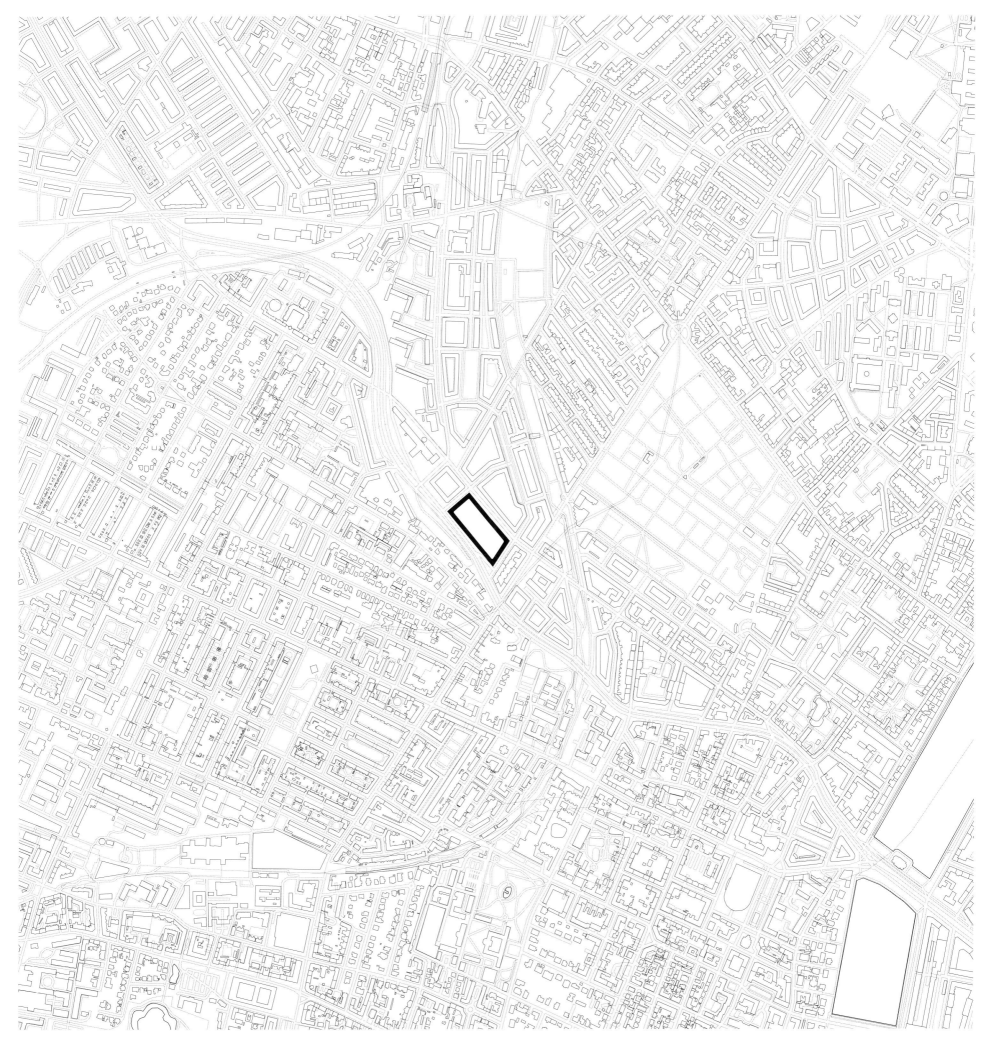

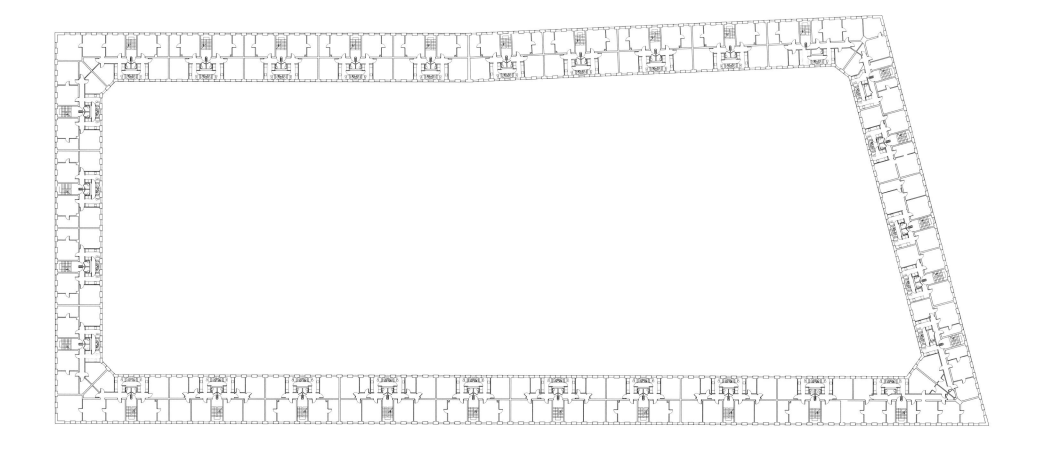

Above: Hornbækhus typical plan – 1:750.
Opposite: Hornbækhus from Borups Allé.

Above: Hornbækhus facade to Borups Allé.
Opposite: Hornbækhus axonometric – 1:750..

44

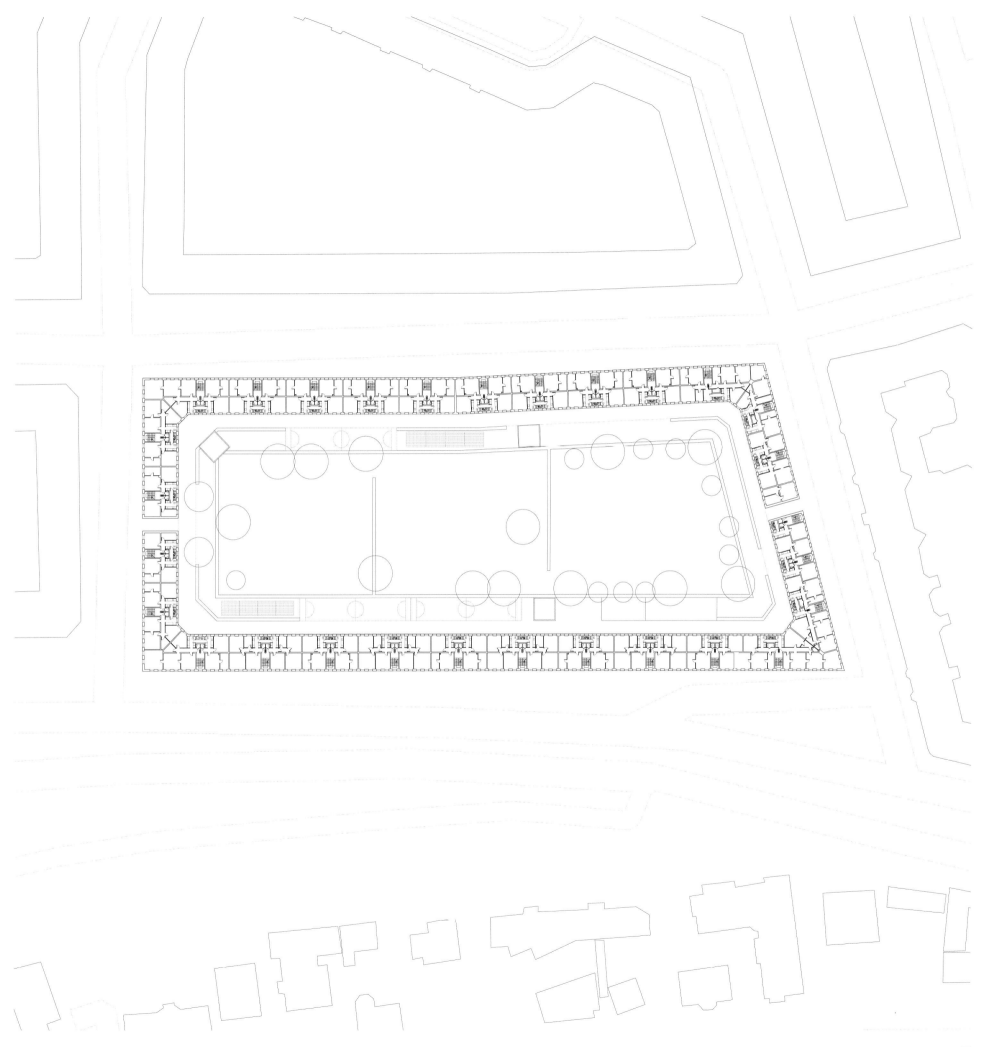

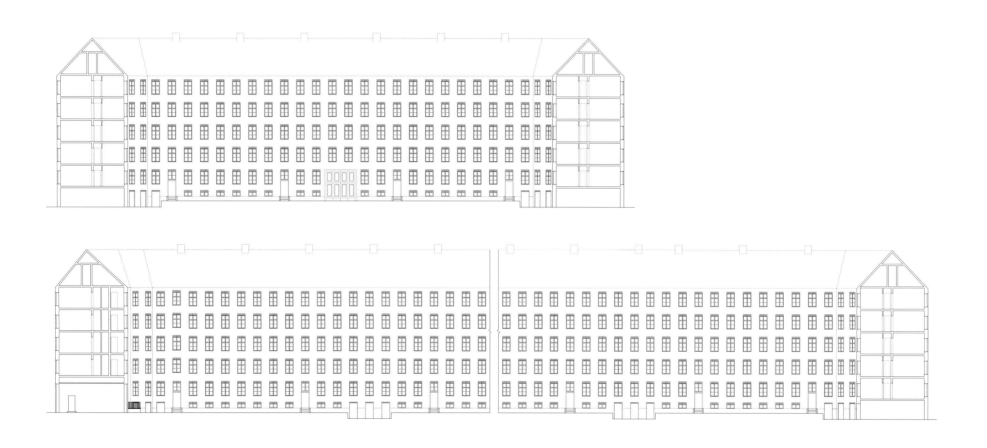

Page 46: Hornbækhus central garden (landscaping not original).
Page 47: Hornbækhus site plan – 1:1000.
Above: Hornbækhus typical sections – 1:500.

Hornbækhus clothes lines.

Hornbækhus facade.

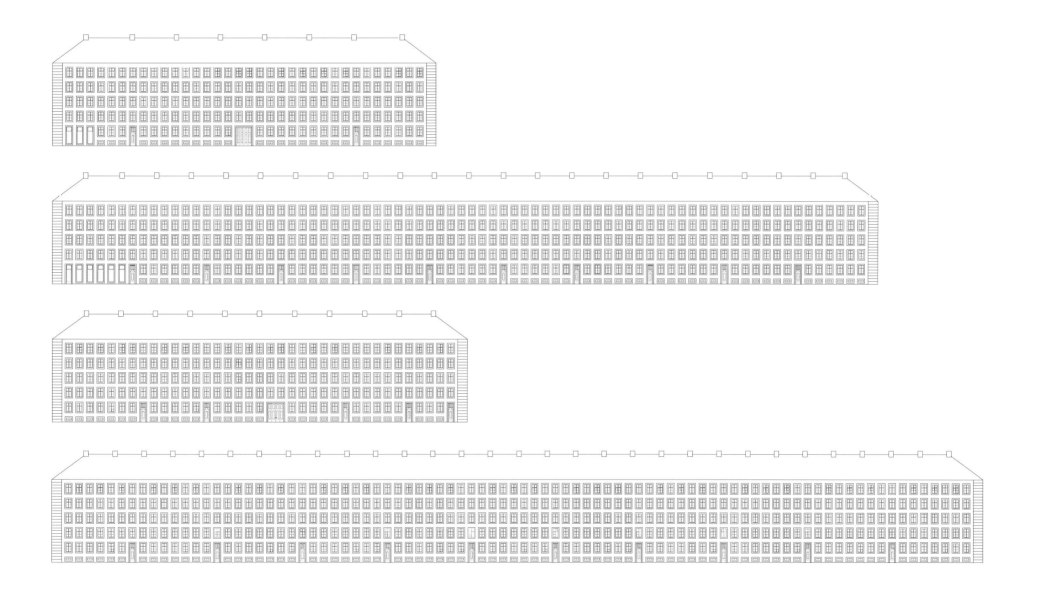

Hornbækhus typical elevations – 1:750.

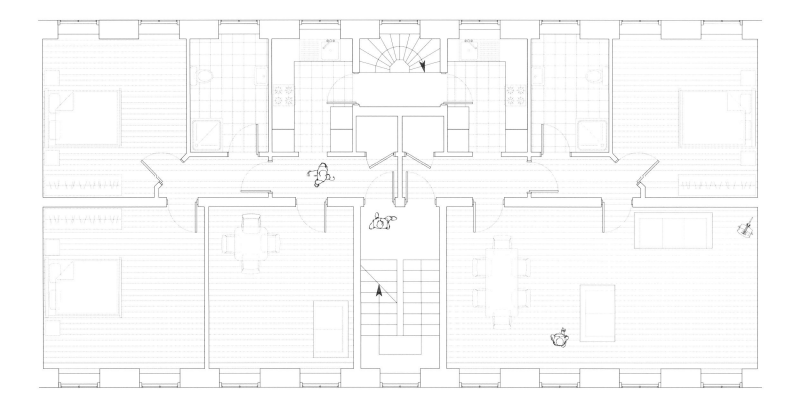

Hornbækhus unit plans – 1:100.

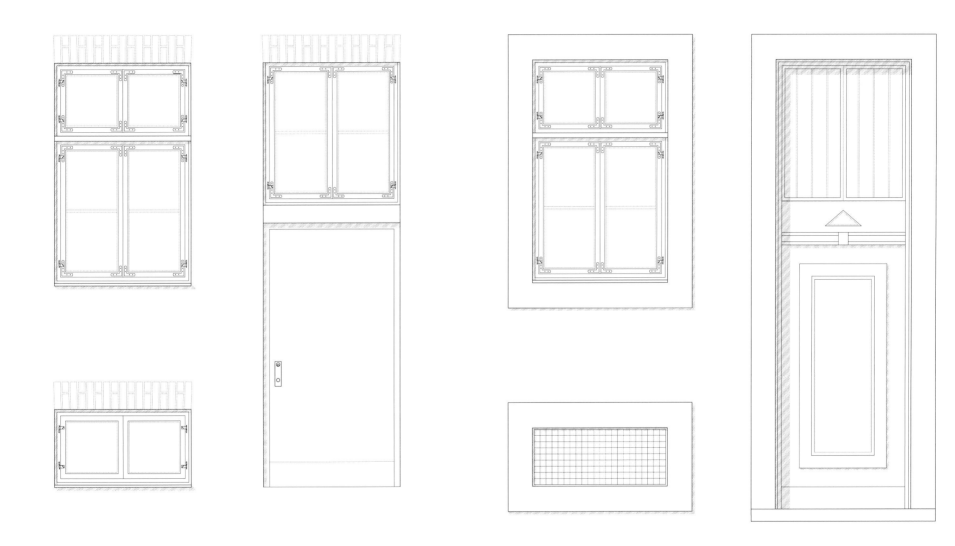

Hornbækhus opening studies – 1:30.

Hornbækhus
Focus: Street and Building

The fabric of the building uses the vernacular of its time: with load-bearing brickwork, timber floors and trussed roof structure. The brick walls are approximately 550mm thick with a narrow cavity and timber or soldier course lintels. The floors are constructed from timber, spanning from exterior wall to internal structural wall. Racking and support for the heavy timber trussed roof is achieved through thicker internal walls spanning from front to back, which rise through the building to purlin level. Constructed from oak, all joints and connections are hole and pegged.

Bespoke construction details were kept to a minimum due to the repetition of the facade; all levels and opening widths are the same.

Hornbækhus detail elevation – 1:50.

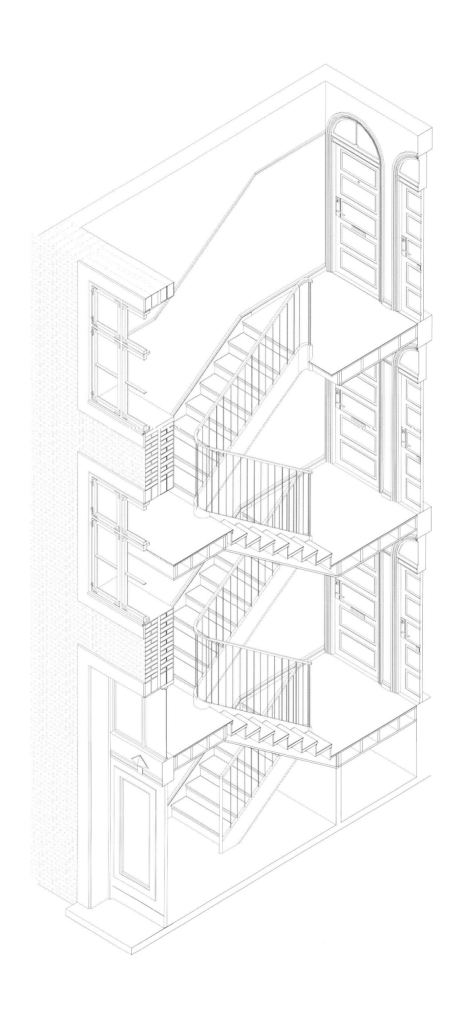

Opposite: entrance door to Hornbækhus
(note lantern coinciding with half-landing).
Above: Hornbækhus detail axonometric – 1:50.

Hornbækhus
Focus: Building and Courtyard

The exterior facades feature a red brick that is much darker than the more rustic yellow brick that is used on the facades facing the courtyard. This softer colour palette on the interior adds to a feeling of calm within the park-sized courtyard.

There are six window variations seen in the project, all based around one window. Within this repetition, small variations have a powerful effect. The outer facades that address the streets always had their future oblique relationship to the city in mind as part of a street. Here, the load-bearing brickwork is subtly dematerialised by the thick plaster bands that surround each window. By expressing the windows forward, the glass catches the light and reflects the surrounding buildings. To the interior courtyard, the plaster band is omitted, the windows puncture the wall and the corners are chamfered to make the buildings embrace softer to the shared garden.

The building's large size does not preclude nuance. Indeed, with the scale offered by this project the tuning of the elevation and of its relief represents the potential for something more. Nuance writ large offers a space for a gentle civic expression.

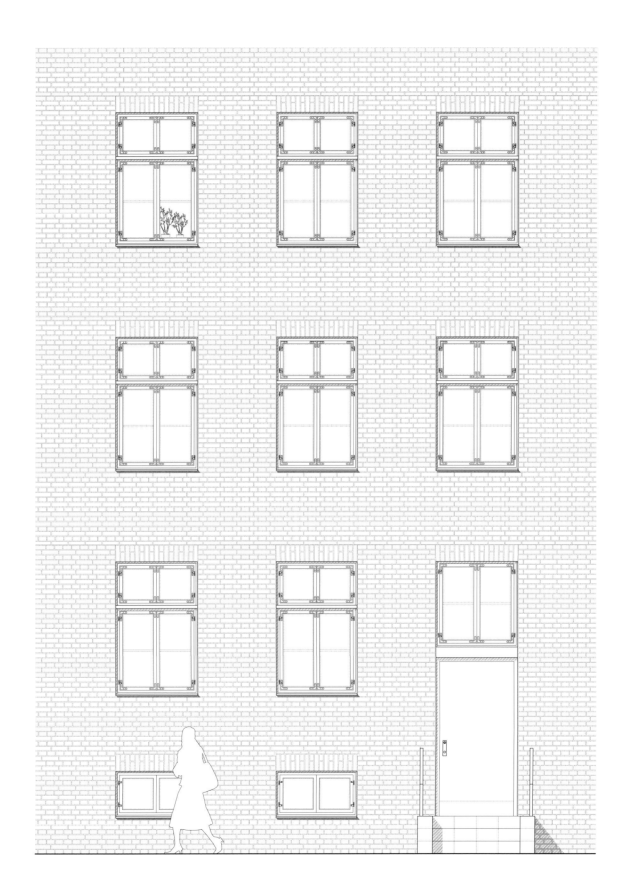

Hornbækhus detail elevation – 1:50 .

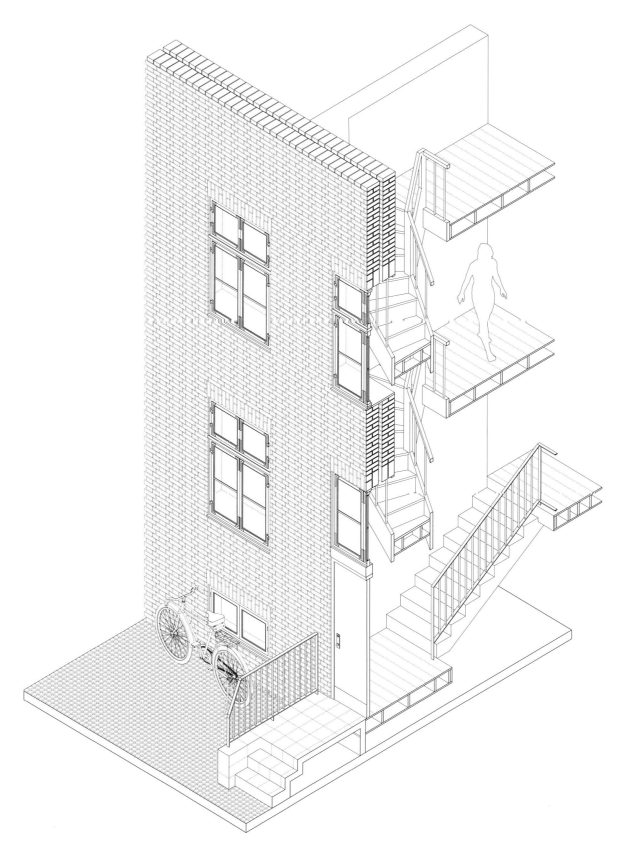

Opposite: Hornbækhus service stairs, with access to the courtyard, effectively giving each apartment a front and back door.
Above: Hornbækhus service stairs detail axonometric – 1:50.

Hornbækhus
Focus: Street and Courtyard

The main window design is a quad casement window with two square, forward-opening sashes at the top and two larger, rectangular, forward-opening sashes at the bottom, all divided by a transom. The paint scheme enhances this subdivision.

Large rectangular windows above the doors are used to match the height of the flanking windows in order to maintain the pattern of the windows across the facade. The windows that provide light into the basement spaces are smaller rectangular windows.

The windows are all made in an identical fashion, with face-mounted steel plates reinforcing each corner and reducing the need to use complex joints or higher grades of timber.

By using the same dimensions throughout, mass production can be applied to reduce the time and cost of fabrication and installation, whilst maintaining the repetitive nature of the project.

Hornbækhus detail elevation – 1:50.

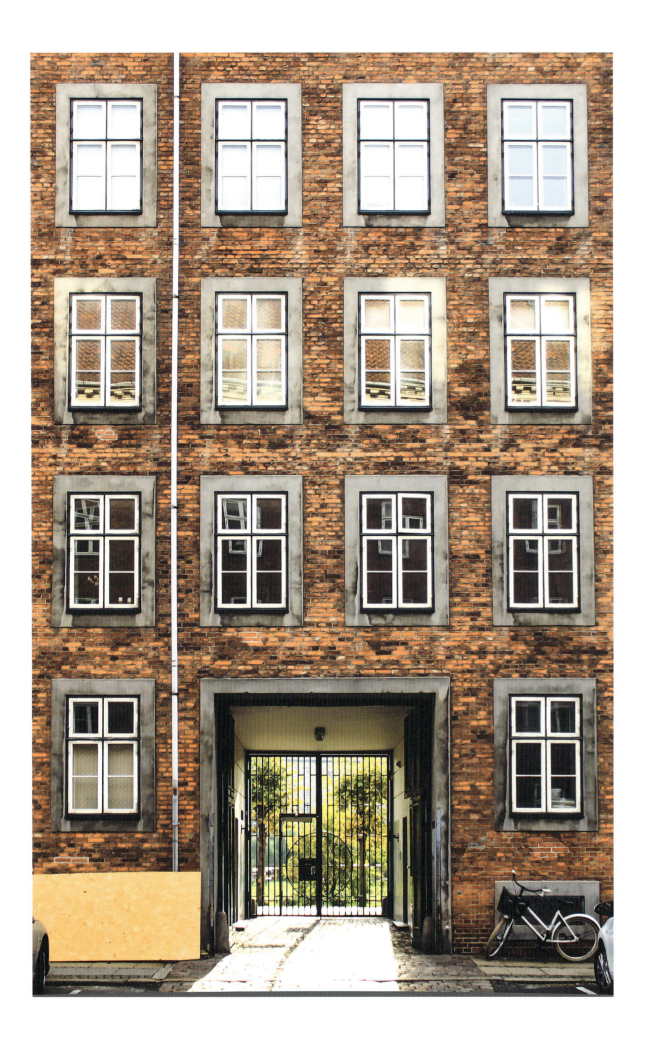

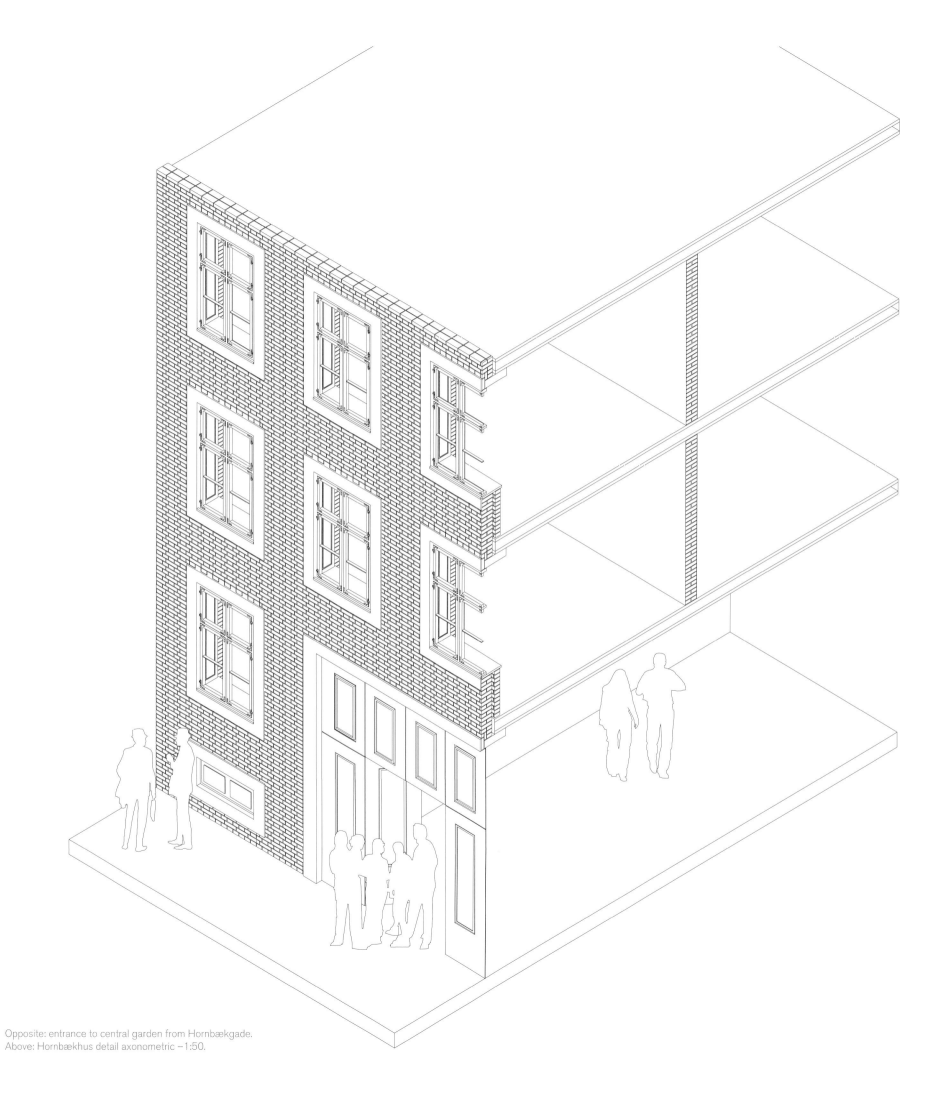

Opposite: entrance to central garden from Hornbækgade.
Above: Hornbækhus detail axonometric –1:50.

Building Study 2: Vestersøhus
'The Terrace'

Vestersøhus, Copenhagen

Student researchers: Kathryn Dowse, Brendan George, Alice Gordon, Brendan Holbeach, Jamie Sloan.

Architects: **Kay Fisker and C.F. Møller**
Completed in phases from **1935 to 1939**

Vestersøhus is set on the site of a former rail station, facing Sankt Jørgens Lake. The client, Anton Nielsen, was a local contractor who also carried out the masonry construction for the project. The long facade was designed to accommodate a seven-storey apartment block containing 264 apartments. The layout of the facades and organisation of the apartments is determined by the north/south position of the building, with the plans ranging from one- to eight-room apartments, grouped around a common staircase.

The semi-recessed balconies are intimately tied to the corner windows, appearing as screens fixed to the flat surface of the facade. The bay-window balcony forms a site of transition between the interior and exterior spaces, and was an innovation that went on to influence many other housing projects. The door to each balcony is placed at the inner corner of the bay window, protected from the weather by the cantilevered balcony above. The south-west orientation of the glass corner provides sunlight from noon to sunset, whilst the low sill height integrates the balcony area visually as well as allowing daylight to reach far into the living room. The balcony is expressed forward as a curved white plane, and it is this weaving of living space, outdoor space and the recessed bedroom that gives the building its civic expression.

Opposite: Vestersøhus location plan – 1:10000.

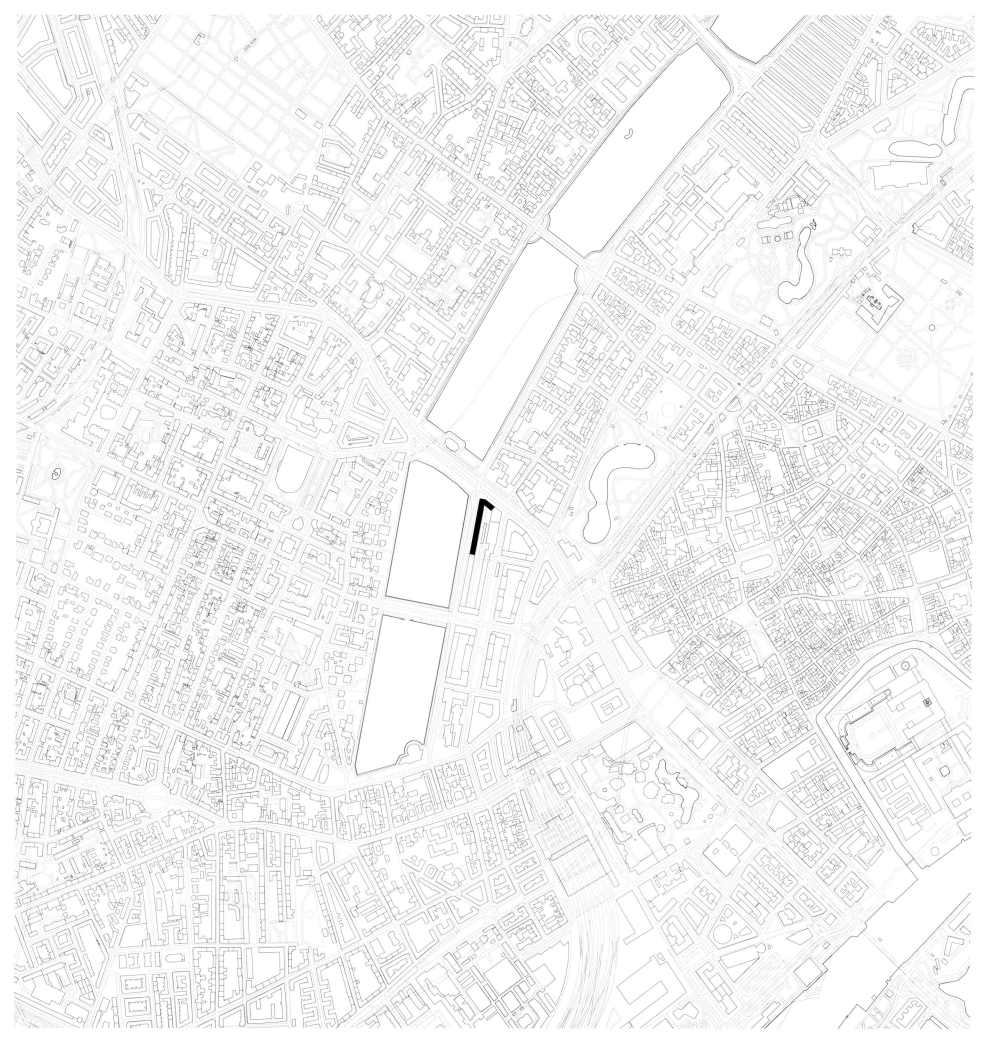

Above: Vestersøhus facade onto Vester Søgade.
Opposite: Vestersøhus axonometric – 1:750.

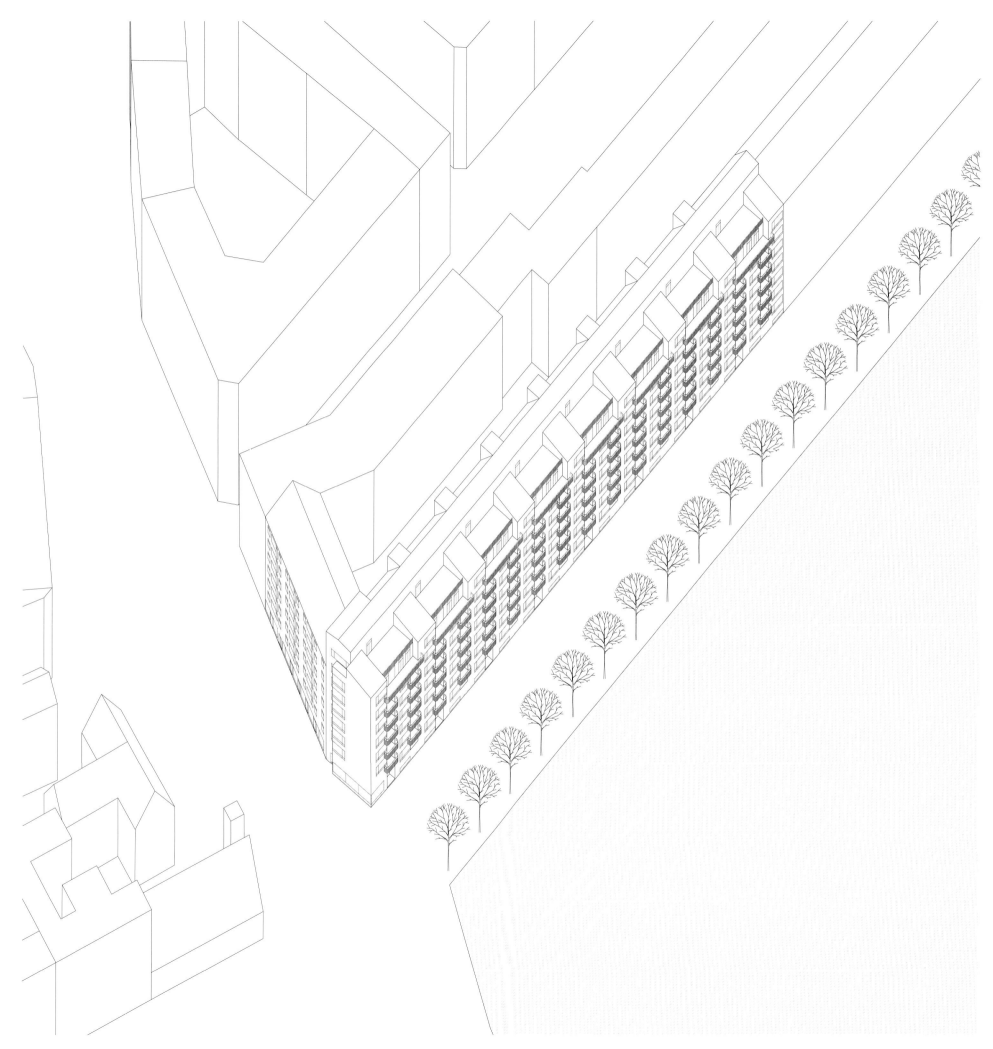

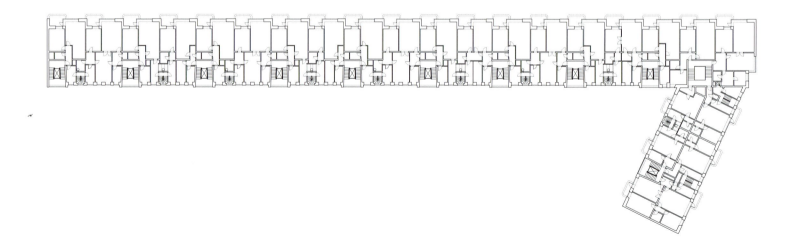

Above: Vestersøhus, view looking south across Peblinge Sø.
Below: Vestersøhus typical plan – 1:750.

Vestersøhus, corner onto Gyldenløvesgade.

Vestersøhus facade viewed from across Sankt Jørgens Sø.

Vestersøhus site plan – 1:1000.

Vestersøhus viewed from across Sankt Jørgens Sø.

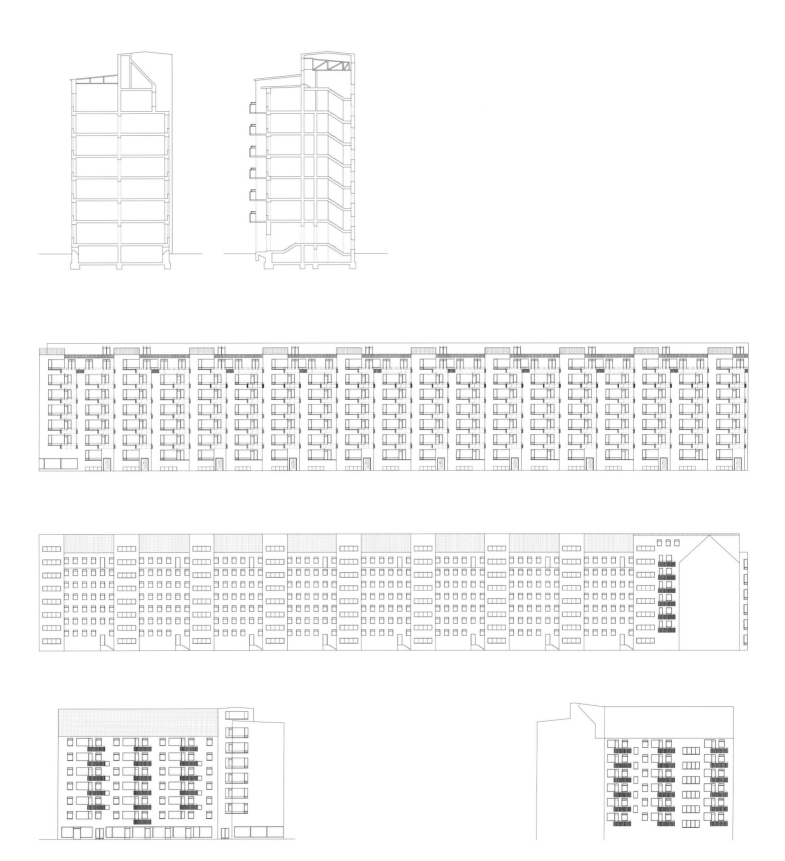

Above: Vestersøhus typical sections – 1:500.
Below: Vestersøhus typical elevations – 1:750.

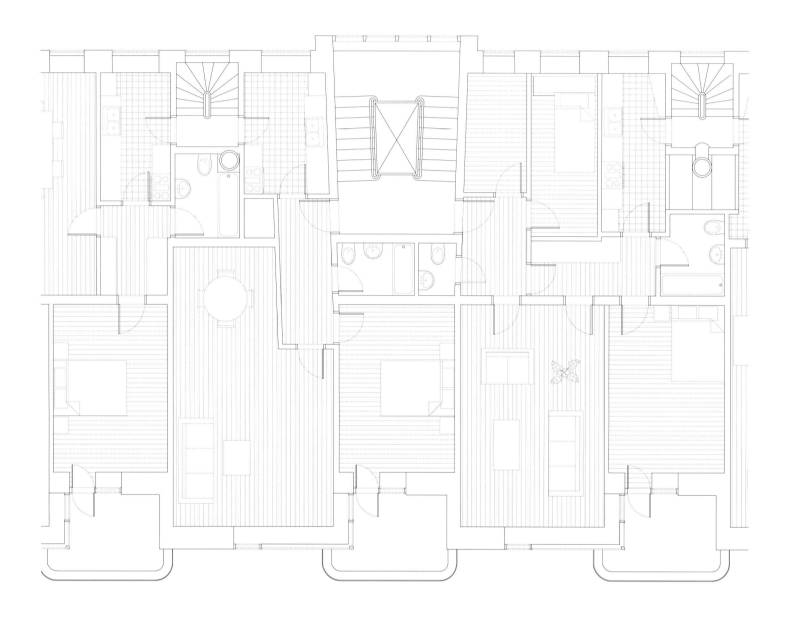

Vestersøhus unit plans – 1:100.

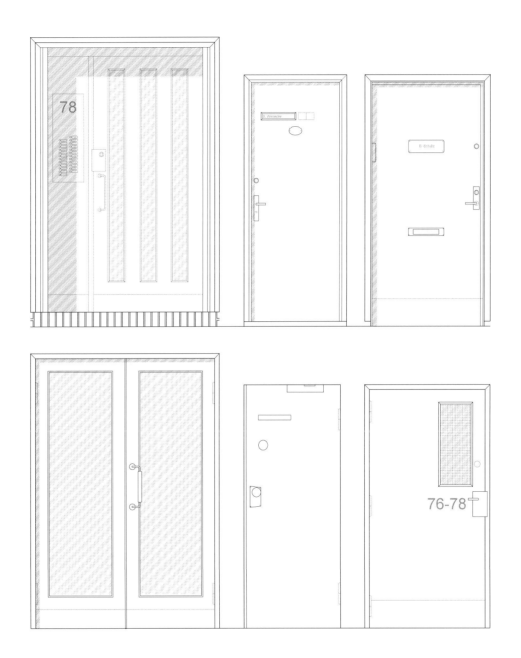

Vestersøhus entrance studies – 1:30.

Vestersøhus
Focus: Threshold

The apartment block was built in two phases: the first phase from 1935–6; and the second phase from 1938–9. A third phase was planned to face the street Nyropsgade but was never executed.

The load-bearing structure and the facades are built as solid masonry construction of red hand-molded bricks. The reinforced concrete floors structurally support the cantilevered balcony and the masonry lintels that bridge across the window openings.

Vestersøhus is possibly one of the most delicate examples of the bay-window balcony housing type developed in Denmark during the 1930s. The entrance to each shared staircase is placed to engage with the lowest level of this arrangement, with the corner windows of these apartments overlooking the doorway to the building. Many of these more public apartments have commercial and professional uses now, including a doctors' surgery and a solicitor's office.

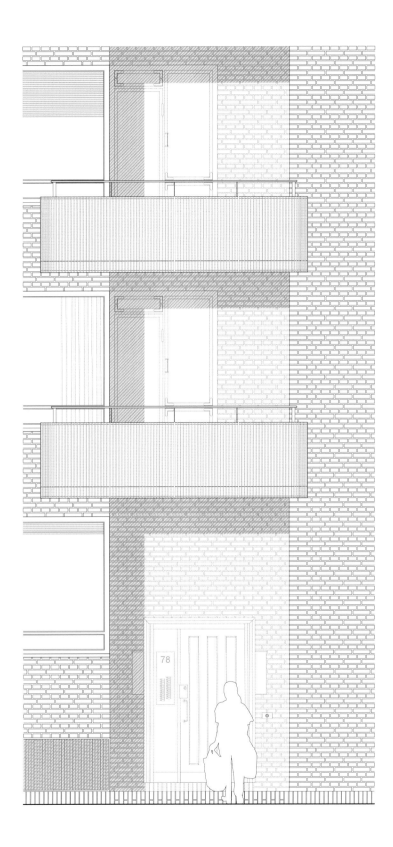

Vestersøhus detail elevation – 1:50.

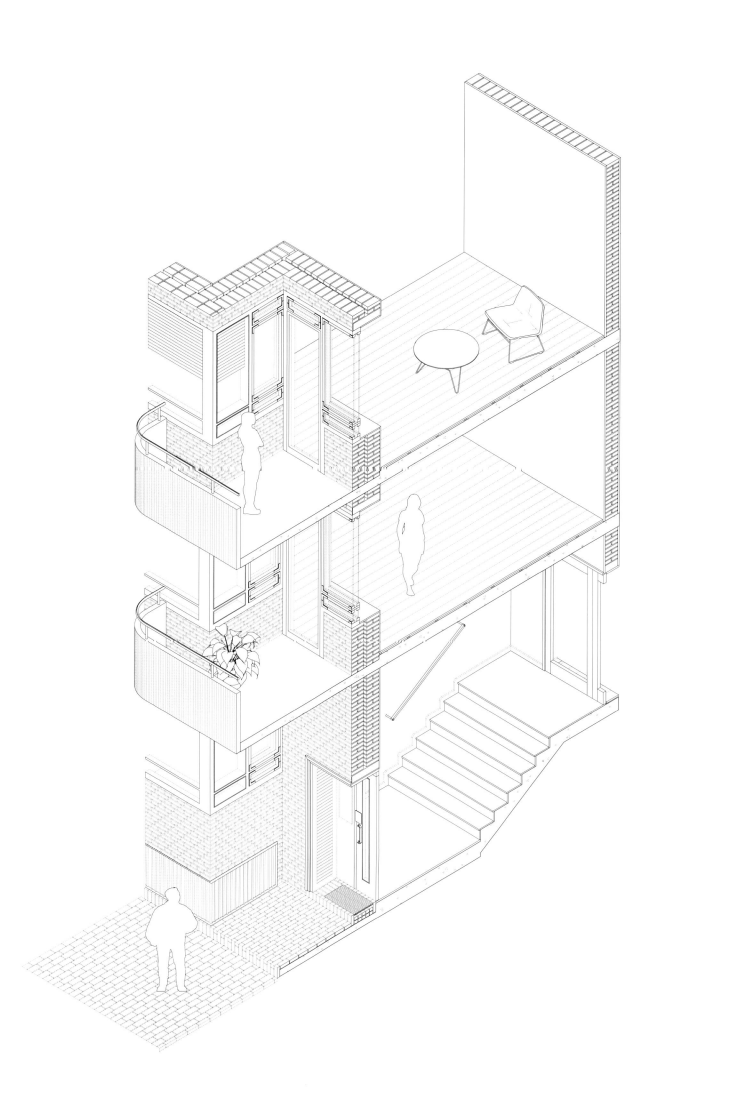

Opposite: Vestersøhus entrance.
Above: Vestersøhus entrance detail
axonometric – 1:50.

Vestersøhus
Focus: Window

The masonry wall becomes an orthogonal relief, holding the same sort of dynamic interplay between light and shadow as is present in the larger design scale of the facade. This material consideration, as well as the spatial qualities, is also emphasised by the windows, which are painted white, juxtaposed against the window frames, which are painted black. The ironwork of the balcony parapets are also painted white, while the grills in front of the basement windows are black.

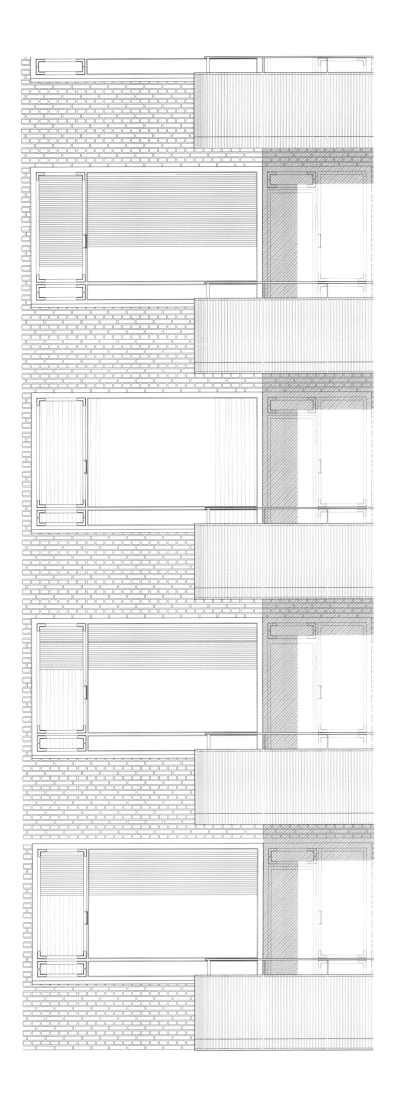

Vestersøhus detail elevation – 1:50.

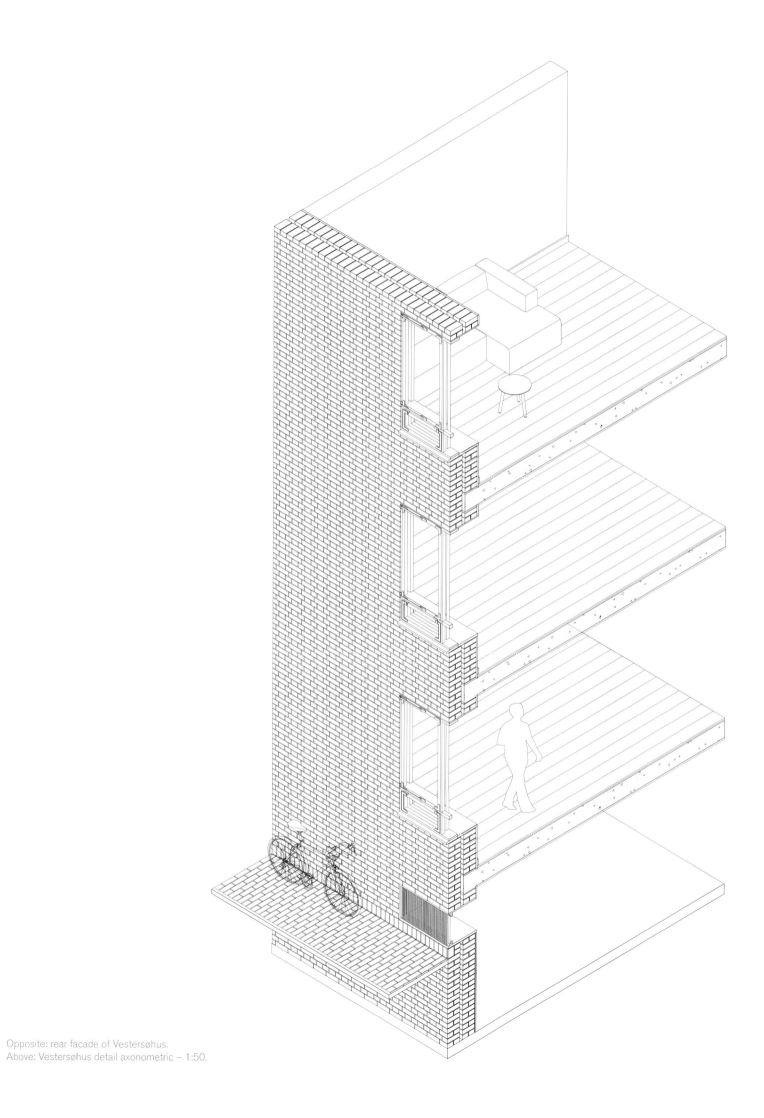

Opposite: rear facade of Vestersøhus.
Above: Vestersøhus detail axonometric – 1:50.

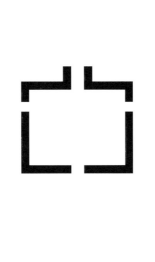

Building Study 3: Dronningegården
'The Square'

Dronningegården

Student researchers: **Matthew Kernan, Magdalena Kisiel, Matthew Lucas, Darragh Sherry, Philippa Southall**

Architects: Kay Fisker, C.F. Møller, Svenn Eske Kristensen
Constructed between 1943 and 1958

The Dronningegården ensemble is situated just outside Copenhagen's historic city centre. The area is part of the partially realised expansion scheme known as 'New Copenhagen' (1650). The urban extension consists of a small grid, with the Dronningens Tværgade axis as the planned link between two public gardens: Kongens Have, a garden for King Frederick III (housing the current Rosenborg Castle) and a garden for Queen Sophie Amalia (where the former summer palace Sophie Amalienborg is located).

In 1943, building began on a new large-scale housing complex along this axis, to replace the dilapidated 17th-century buildings. This new addition, designed by Kay Fisker in the shape of a large quadrangle, restores the connection between Kongens Have park and Sophie Amalienborg.

This quadrangle was proposed by Fisker as an 'outdoor living room', scaled to echo Amalienborg square. In his early impressions of the scheme, Fisker depicted the courtyard as a park. However, at present, the courtyard is used for car-parking and does not function as the green foyer he envisioned.

The complex features 72 apartments per floor and 20 vertical circulation points. The ground floor on Borgergade consists of commercial spaces topped by eight floors and approximately 624 apartments.

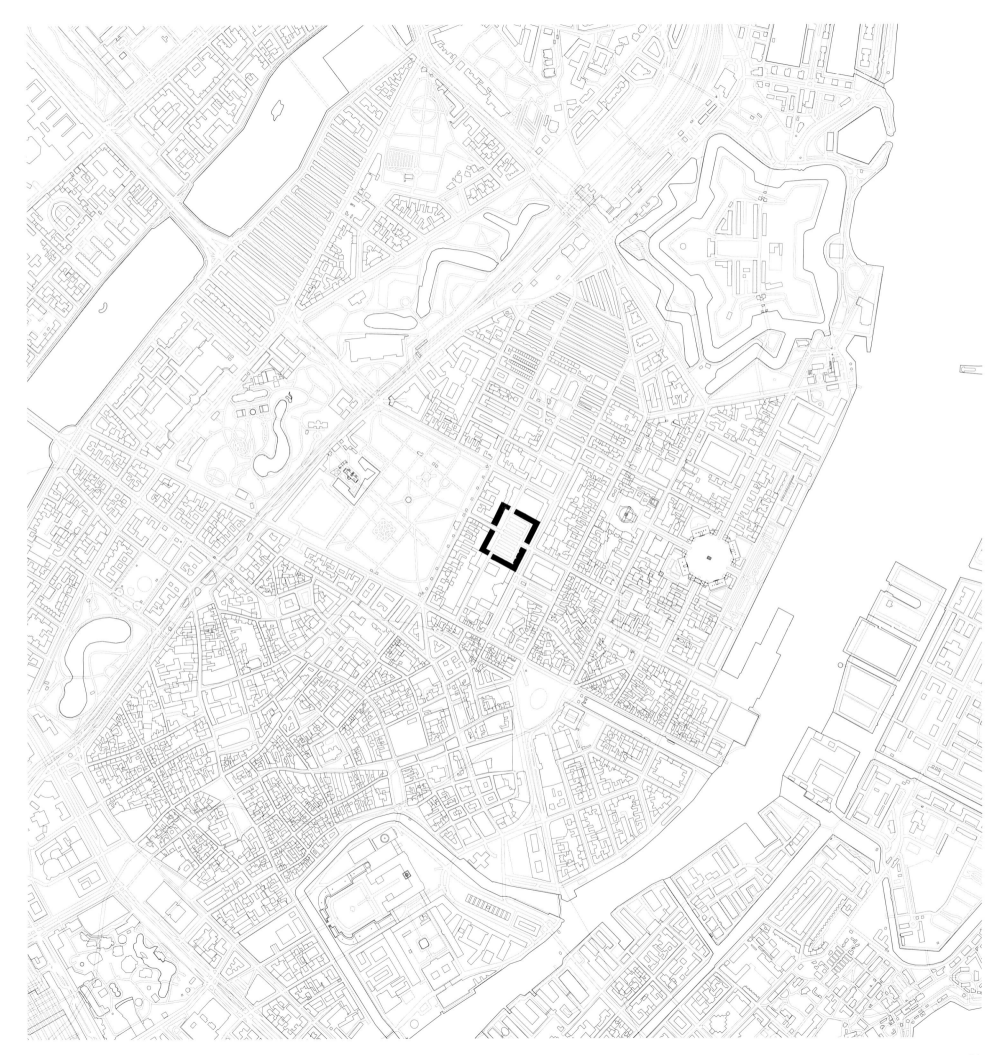

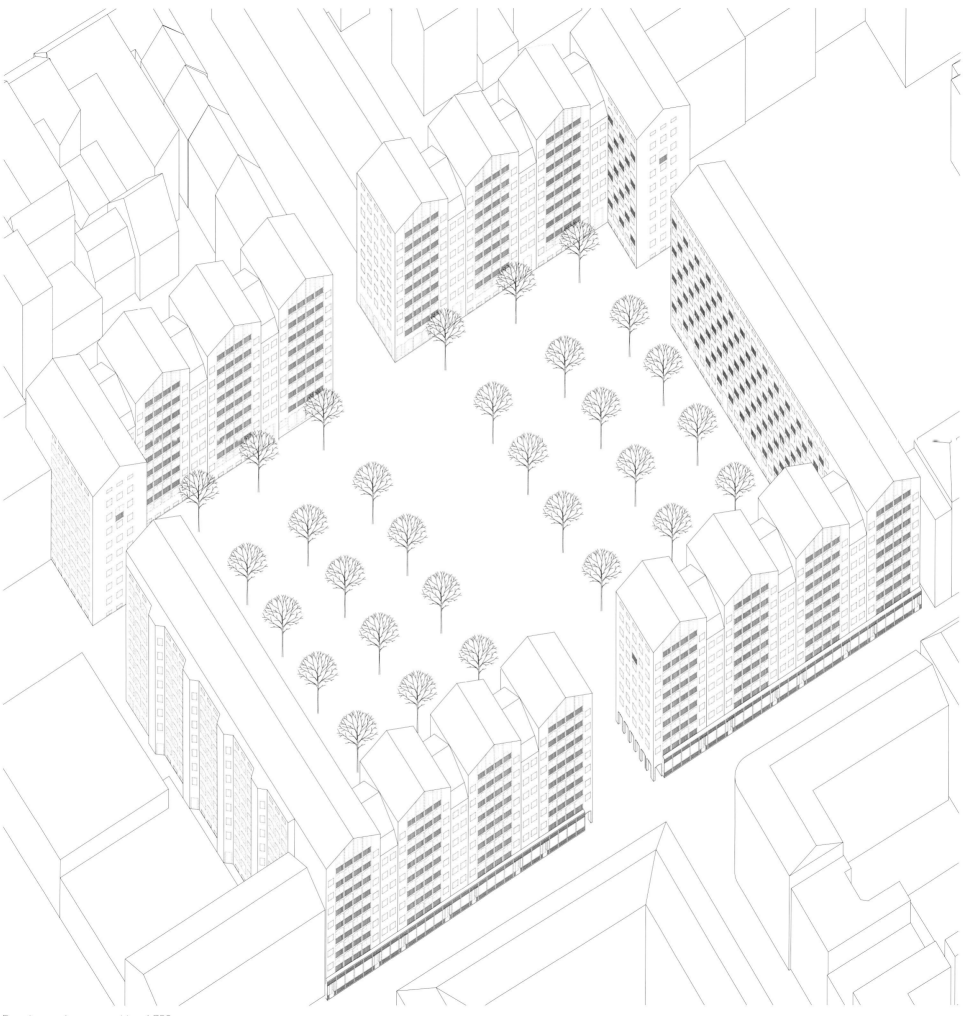
Dronningegården axonometric – 1:750.

Opposite: Dronningegarden site plan – 1:1000.

94

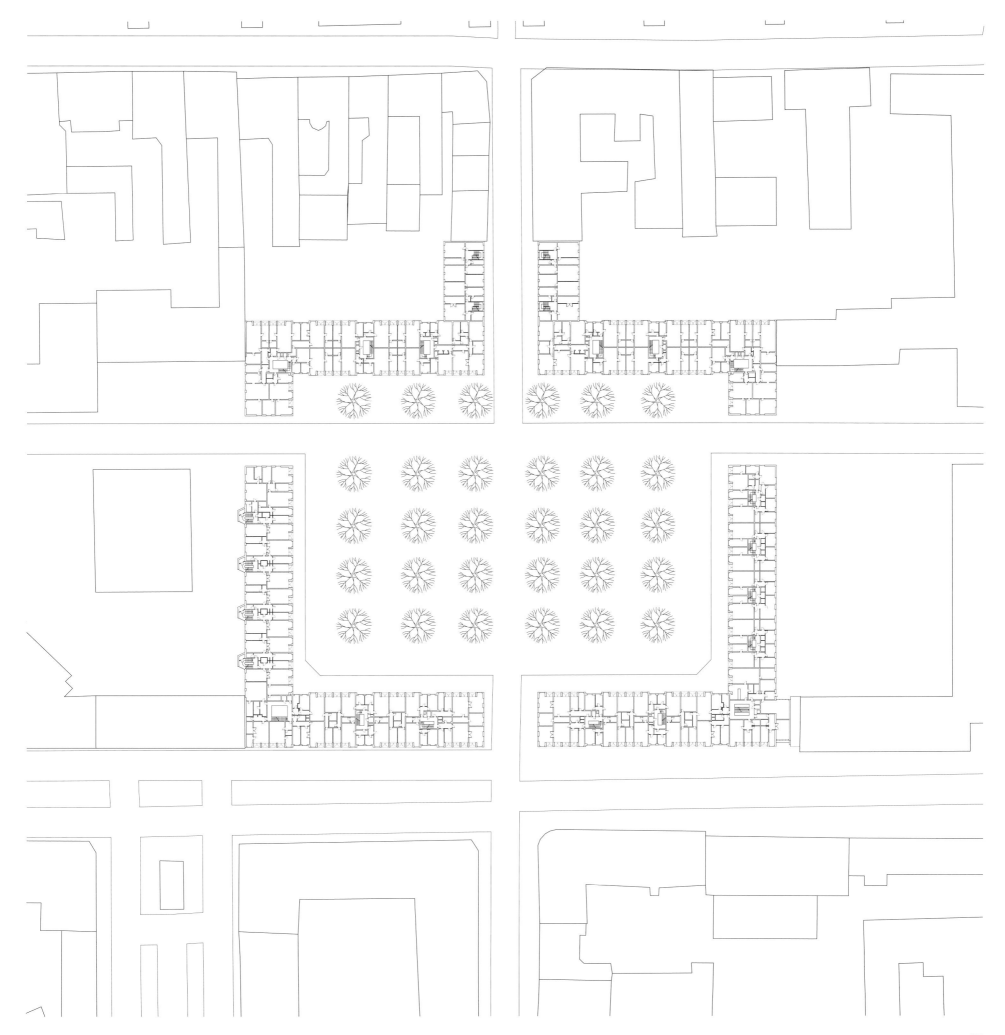

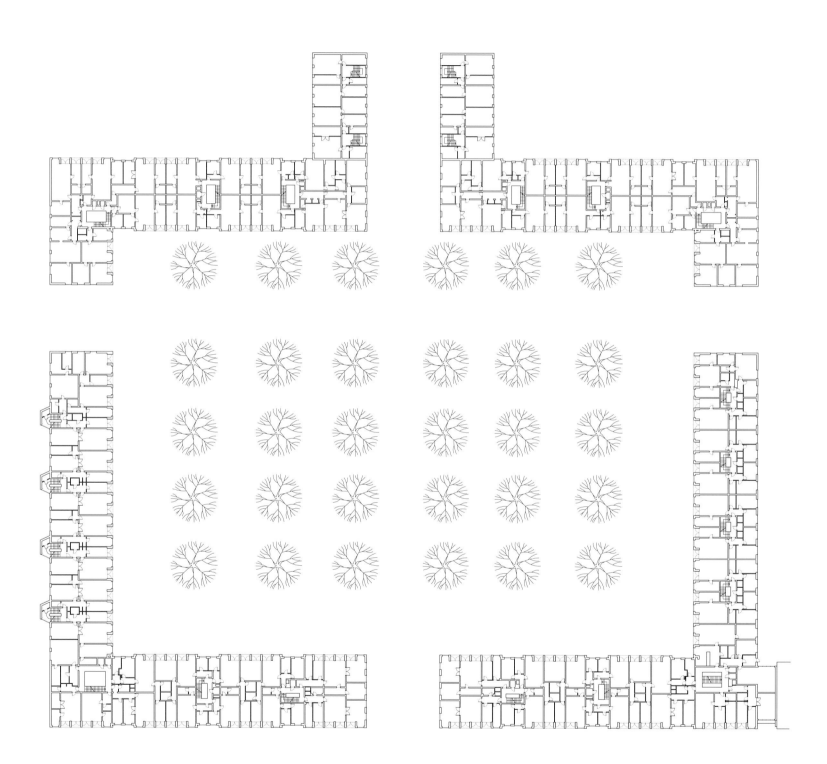

Dronningegarden typical plan – 1:750.

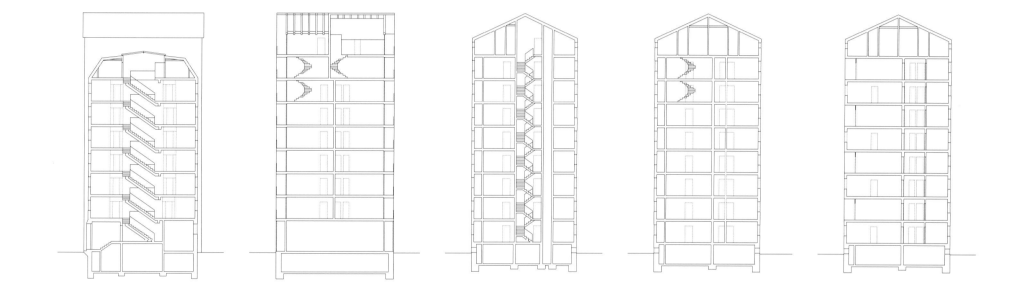

Dronningegarden typical sections – 1:500.

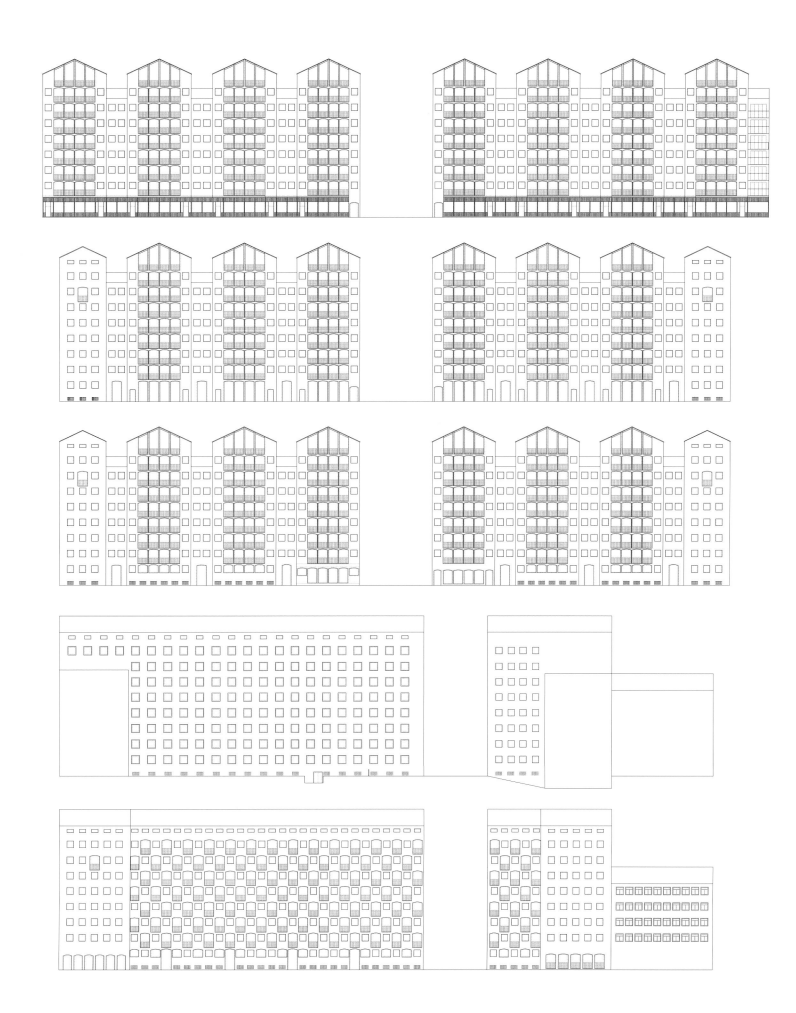

Dronningegarden typical elevations – 1:750.

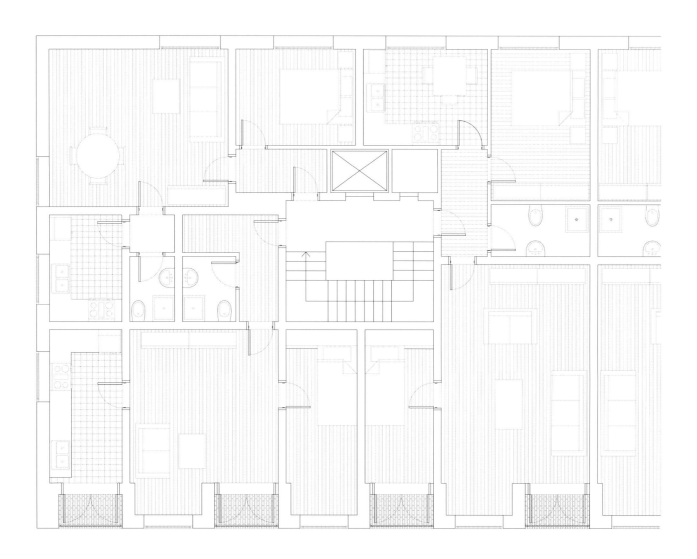

Dronningegarden unit plans – 1:100.

Dronningegarden balcony studies – 1:30.

Dronningegården
Focus: Relief

The quadrangle is a collection of four volumes, each of which is designed differently to respond to the diverse conditions of their surroundings. Window and balcony types are simple elements that are repeated in patterns that modulate each facade, working at the scale of the city and detail at the same time.

The north and south volumes that address the inner quadrangle are composed of a unique alternating window balcony arrangement, illustrated here.

Dronningegården detail elevation – 1:50 .

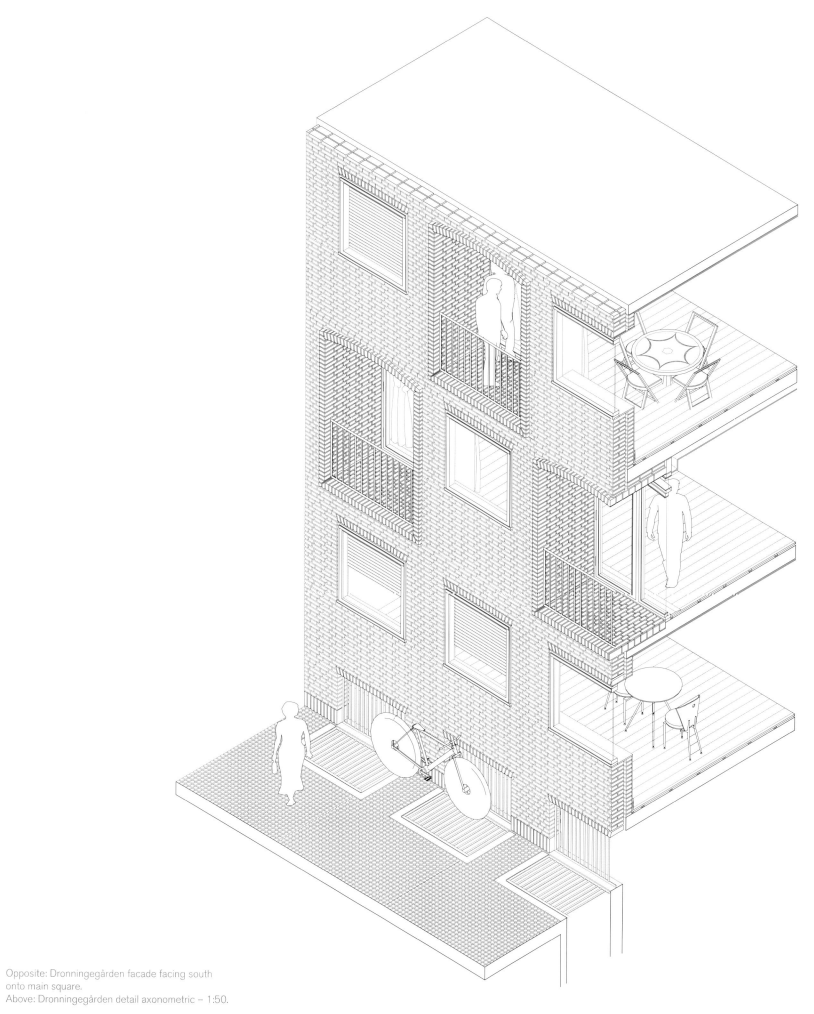

Opposite: Dronningegården facade facing south onto main square.
Above: Dronningegården detail axonometric – 1:50.

105

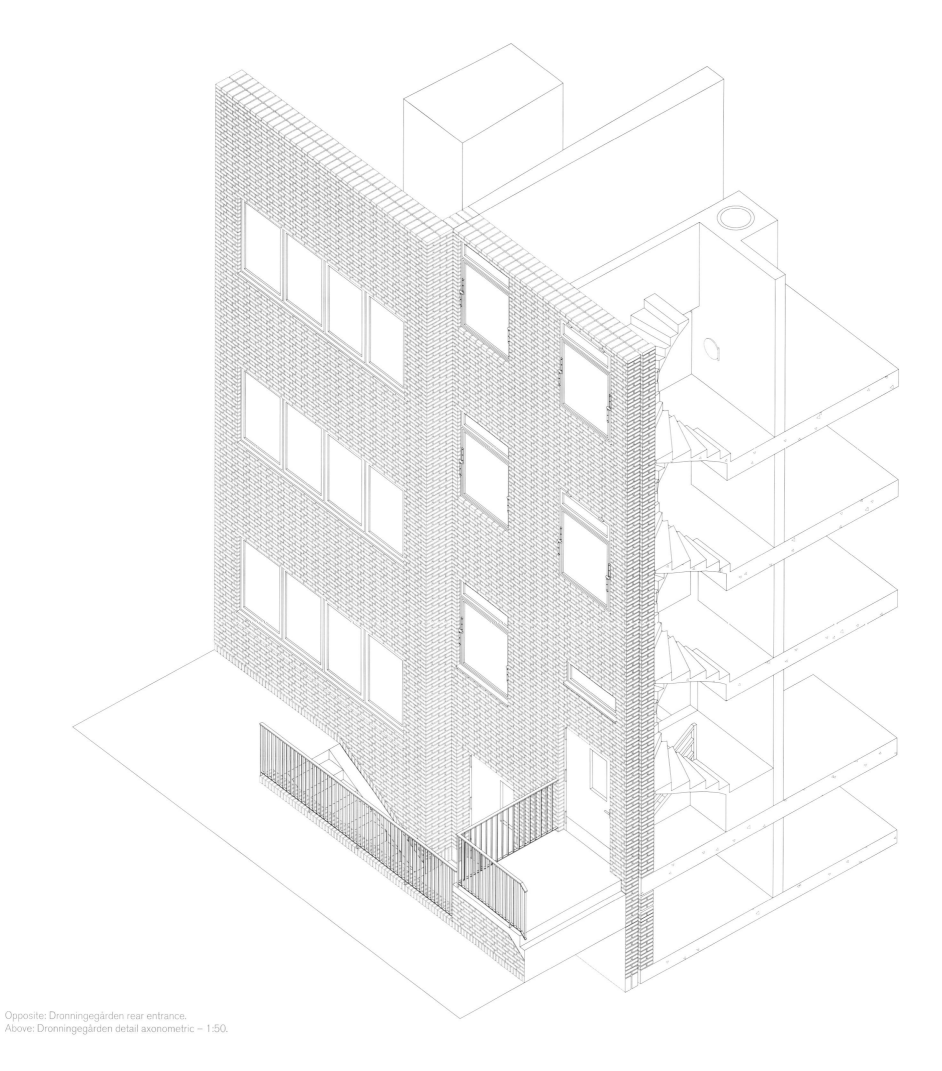

Opposite: Dronningegården rear entrance.
Above: Dronningegården detail axonometric – 1:50.

Dronningegården
Focus: Threshold

The details of the brickwork allow the larger scale of the blocks to be tuned to the individual inhabitant. A subtle pattern in the bond becomes legible when close to the building. Specials are used to make reveals to doorways.

Dronningegården detail elevation – 1:50.

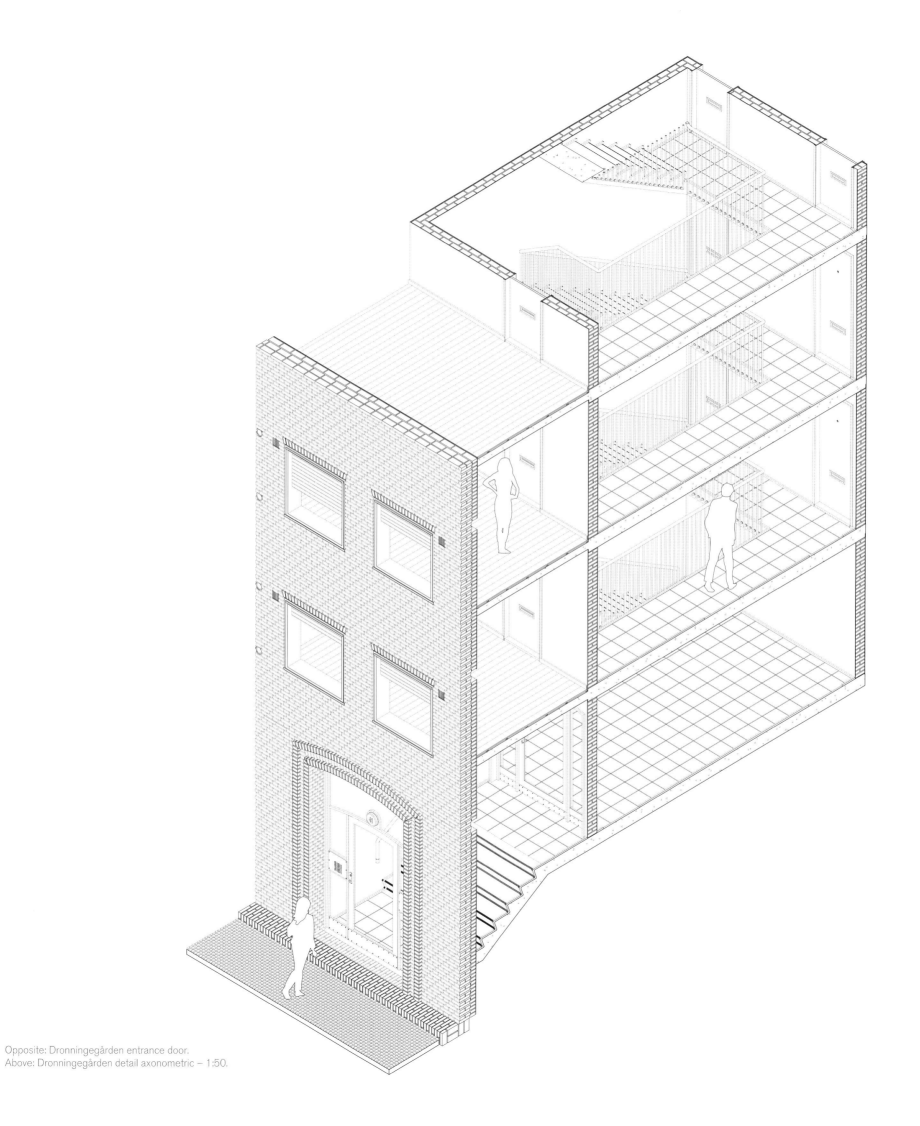

Opposite: Dronningegården entrance door.
Above: Dronningegården detail axonometric – 1:50.

111

Dronningegården
Focus: Puncture

The strict repetition of window openings and balconies, set in stripped-down facades, creates a basic rhythm. The disposition and depth of the openings are modulated to make balconies and windows.

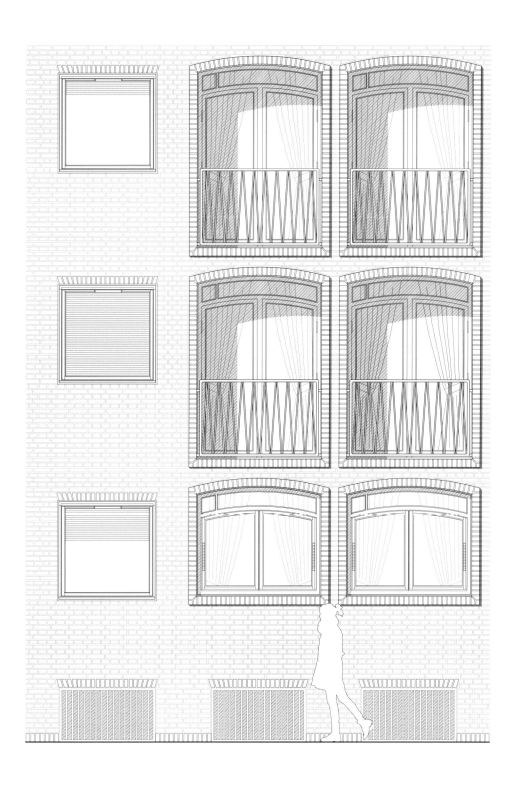

Dronningegården detail elevation – 1:50.

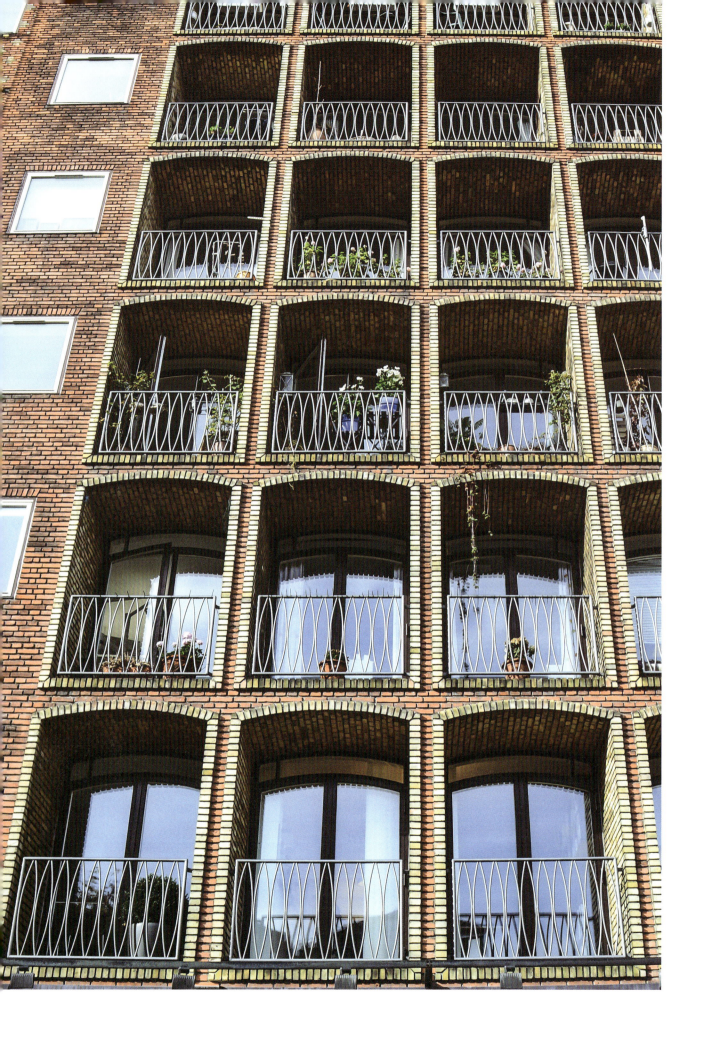

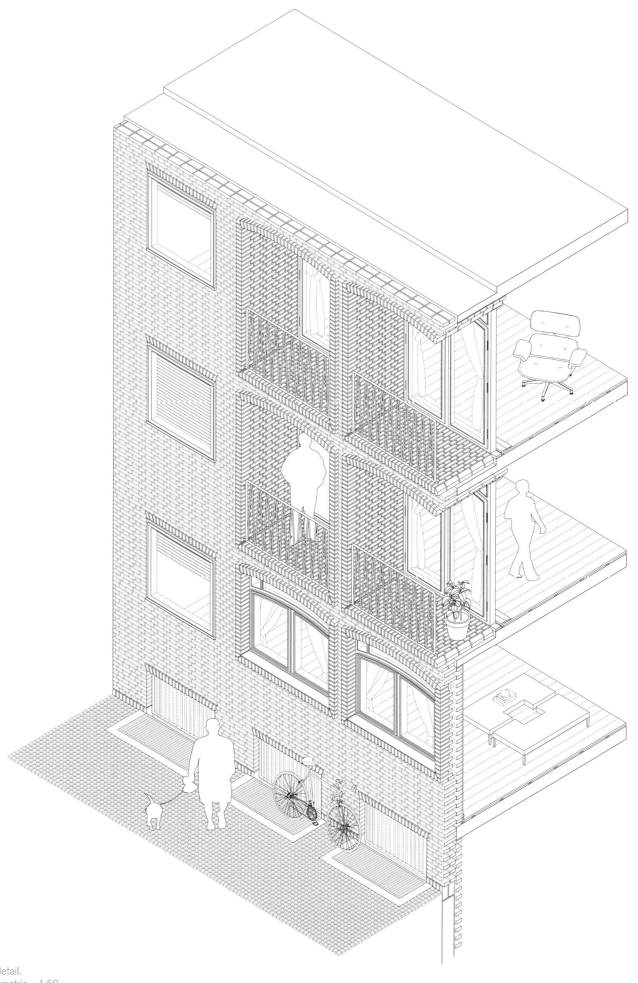

Opposite: Dronningegården balcony detail.
Above: Dronningegården detail axonometric – 1:50.

The Moral of Functionalism

Kay Fisker

First published as the article 'Funktionalismens Moral' in *A5 Meningsblad for unge arkitekter 3*, no.4, 1947, pp 7–14. Republished as 'The Moral of Functionalism' in *Magazine of Art* 2, 1950, pp 62–7.

Reprinted with kind permission of the Estate of Kay Fisker.

During these post war years, eager attempts are being made to wind up the estate of functionalism. The logical conclusion of this is that functionalism must be dead, and this is no doubt correct so long as we look upon functionalism as a style. Its programme, nonetheless includes more than the short lived period characterised by functionalist ideals of form. Functionalism holds a moral that is eternal: the demand for functional architecture. Lately there seems to be a tendency towards a slackening of this demand; but it is important that it should be maintained and fulfilled during the years to come.

The victory of functionalism put an end to the prevailing eclecticism. During the nineteenth century, the historical approach to architecture had become so firmly anchored that it was maintained for the greater part of a century, in spite of changes in cultural pattern, the progress of democracy and liberalism, the emergence of strong and independent artistic personalities among the architects and the extensive technical and industrial development that had taken place.

Eclectic architecture is formal: concern with form supersedes all other demands. Custom, technique and social conditions are considered only in the light of a previously fixed ideal of form. No correspondence is demanded between contents and expression; the outer shell becomes a garment, a mask, without connection with the interior. "Architecture is a decoration of constructions", said Sir Gilbert Scott, the main figure within the English gothic revival. A striking feature of the period was that completely new construction methods, due to the development of industrialism, arose without immediately being given outward expression. Industrialisation brought about the standardisation of the various parts of a building and eventually produced architectural innovations of a revolutionary nature. The architects of the Renaissance and baroque worked on a principle of form whereby the house was constructed, almost modelled, as a whole; but industrialism entailed the building of a house out of fabricated parts which were then fitted into a whole. In the childhood of industrialism, these standard parts were made without reference to the nature of materials or to their effect on construction. Carried away by the new technical possibilities, people tended to forget there were essential differences between plaster and cast iron. The material existed only to be painted, not for any intrinsic merit, and forms were taken from architectural history. But while apparently the form was borrowed, in fact a whole new principle of form was created.

Functionalism was to carry this principle of form to its logical conclusion. New technical methods and new possibilities of construction, though often romanticised beyond their importance, were the most important influence in this evolution. The products of machine production - the ship, the automobile and the aeroplane - became the models, and steel and reinforced concrete served to create the new forms. In the nineteenth century, iron had made its appearance as a quite new element in architecture; but only a few architects like Labrouste and Sullivan permitted it to become an artistic part of their construction. In the twentieth century reinforced concrete introduced an architectural factor that combined the massive qualities of masonry with the tensile strength of iron or steel. Sometimes design was dictated wholly by construction, as in Russian architecture of the early days of the Soviet Republic. Construction then became an end

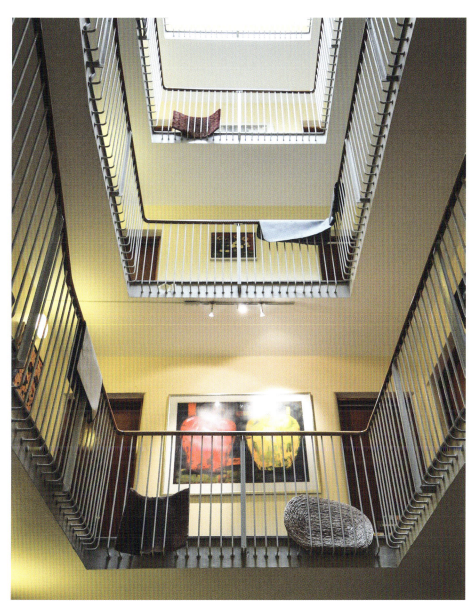

Dronningegården interior.

in itself, as well as the mans: Tatlin's design (1920) for a monument to the third international in Moscow is a large iron-grille structure with no content or expression other than its construction.

The space principles presented by functionalism as radically new also had their roots in the preceding century. Let us consider one development of the 1850s having to do with the formation of the house plan. In England, eclecticism brought about a special cultivation of the gothic tradition which led to a break with the established forms of classicism, at least so far as the dwelling was concerned. The English house plan of the 1850s broke completely with the French equivalent of the "railroad flat" type of plan which formerly prevailed. Large suites disappeared; efforts were made to avoid the necessity of passing through each room to reach another, and to make each room as self-contained and private as possible. Convenience, spaciousness, division of the plan according to the use of the rooms, orientation for sunlight, ventilation and the best view - all these were considered more important than symmetry, regularity and monumentality, indeed even more important than the architectural proportions of the rooms, window bays and building elements. Thus the plan became free and irregular, with rooms grouped around a large, often two storied central room.

The shape and disposition of our rooms today is based on logical adaptions of this point of view. In the modern house, exterior and interior are no longer separate conceptions but merge into each other. As early as the 1890s, Frank Lloyd Wright has made use of this principle, and Le Corbusier has varied the theme in many ways. His architecture has often been described as a composition of cubical and cylindrical blocks. This is a misconception: his architecture is composed of flat surfaces and an interaction between interior and exterior; its constituents are not volumes but wall-diagrams enclosing space within which the rooms flow into one another. Often a large central room occupies several stories and ramifies into secondary rooms, while the whole interior is separated from the surrounding greenery only by a glass wall. The connection with the English house design of the past century here is evident, and the development has proceeded with convincing logic.

The same thing may be said of even that more popular side of functionalism: its social aspect. This, too, represents an advance in a development originating in England. Principles employed first in houses of the rich were soon applied to houses for the population at large, and functionalism found itself concerned with the plain standard dwelling that constitutes 80 per cent of all house building. While functionalism's aesthetic language of form often aroused violent resistance, its social programmes almost from the outset met with general sympathy. Een those who were irritated by flat roofs and large windows found the social endeavours of the young architects praiseworthy and approved of their preoccupation with the solution of the problem of the house rather than with monumental building. This duty of the architect to serve the community was a convincing argument in any discussion. Yet even this aspect had begun with liberalism, a generation or two before.

Thus although functionalism was set forth as a violently revolutionary movement, so far its basic tenets were concerned it would have been more natural had its course been continuous and evolutionary. In social and technical forces as well as in planning, the origins of functionalism has all been present in the nineteenth century. Only the language of form had lagged behind. By the end of the century however, a few architects in widely operated parts of the world had made scattered and independent attempts to advance beyond style to a logical, more honest architecture, with accord between form and purpose. They were fighting for reason and humanity. "Form follows function" was Louis Sullivan's doctrine in the 1880s; "houses for people to live in" was Baillie Scott's programme; in 1902, Henry even de Velde lectured on Vernunftgemäße Schönheit (logical beauty); in 1906, CFA Voysey wrote of "reason as a basis of art"; Stilarchitektur oder Baukunst (traditional architecture or the art of building) was the choice with which Hermann Muthesius confronted his age in a propaganda publication of 1912.

Many of the solutions arrived at by these men, under the influence of their own times, are misunderstood now, but the foundation on which they built was surely the right one, and the one on which the men of the 1920s were to build further. Of these pioneers, seventy-five year old Auguste Perret and eighty year old Frank Lloyd Wright are still active and are still faced with great tasks. Perret is rebuilding Le Havre, and Wright still confronts us with new and strange solutions. But both are the children of their own generation. In spite of his pioneer constructions, Peret is firmly anchored in Beaux-Arts Classicism, and Wright has never discarded the ornamental principles of Louis Sullivan and Otto Wagner. Wright's field, however is wider than his teachers: he loves and cultivates the raw materials of nature. He is the reformer of the community,

Vestersøhus interior.

who still believes in Ruskin and Morris and who works towards decentralisation and a close connection with the soil. His ideas of town planning, by which every man is to own his own land, are the realisation of Thomas Jefferson's first democratic manifestos of 1776 and have their roots deep in the philosophy of the American colonists.

Unlike Perret and Wright, Le Corbusier and Gropius speak the language of our time. They are as different from one another as they are different from Wright. Functionalism has been greatly enriched by the interaction of these three: Wright, the Angle-Saxon nature-romantic; Le Corbusier, the Latin machine-romantic; and the Germanic and socially-minded Walter Gropius, impelled by the romance of logic.

Le Corbusier is the artist, and his accent is ever on the aesthetic. He says: "man has forged a new tool… Nothing in nature approaches the perfection with which the machine is able to create. Instead of the but imperfectly round orange, the machine produces balls, cones and cylinders cut with precision never shown to us by nature. The work is so wonderful as to awaken new senses within us… The house should be regarded as a machine to live in…" All his writings are characterised by a lyric tone; the heart of his point of view lies in its aesthetic nature. But his genius is indisputable.

The Bauhaus School of Gropius fought for social understanding and for rationalism in the creation of forms: the so called Neue Sachlichkeit. It regarded romantic nonsense all values except those dictated by considerations of technique, economy, analysis of function and use, easy maintenance and durability; artistic content was forced into the background. The designation of Baukunst was replaced by Bauen; the architectural schools were renamed the Building Schools; and the architect would have preferred to exchange his title for that of engineer. Naturally appreciation for architecture of the past faded, and architecture as an art could only be mentioned in cautions circumlocutions. Admittedly he study of the art of buildings in previous ages is our best guide for the teaching of form, but it must be seen against the social and cultural background of its time and not, as in periods of eclecticism, be regarded as a basis for imitation. The architecture of the past should be studied as the classical scholar studies Latin: not in order to speak the language but to understand its structure and coherence.

Functionalism was a cleansing agent which swept over nations like a storm, liberating and stimulating. It was necessary, but it destroyed too much. Architecture became skeletal, sterile and antiseptic. At times the whole movement seemed inhuman. Reaction grew: not the reaction that called forth politically influenced styles of architecture, such as the dilettante classicism of Nazism and the monumentalised Cubism of fascism, but a spontaneous reaction throughout the world against the penurious, the puristic and the over-simplified. Undoubtedly this was caused by fuctionalism's apparent arbitrary creation of form, even though this may have been based on an honest accord between exterior and interior. A need was felt for richness, for artistic imagination, for order in architecture. Symmetry and monumentality were not necessary, but architecture must have as well a rhythm of orderly arrangement, corresponding to the joints of the body, the acts of a drama, the movements of a symphony or the chapters of a book.

During the post war years we have been groping towards an answer. The war has shaken many of us so fundamentally that it seems impossible to pick up the thread from the remote prehistoric days of 193. Catastrophe has left us uncertain and suspicious; we no longer know in what to believe. In some places architects have reverted to historic forms. In Holland and Warsaw former leaders of extreme functionalism are now designing large structures influenced by the Baroque, and in France Beaux-Arts classicism has again come to the fore. The immediate direction of this development is unimportant, for reactionary tendencies have been present in every age. What should alarm us is the fact that those very architects who formerly helped to promote functionalism are not searching over other ideals.

Less alarming, but no more positive, are the attempts to make functionalism more palatable through decoration and other camouflage. 'Ornament is always placed to conceal a misconstruction', said Le Corbusier. Evidently that point of view is not that of the present time. Young architects are writing articles about the coldness of functionalism which must be mitigated through ornamentation. A desire is spreading for decoration, sometimes of a purely external nature, groping and helpless. Often the actual decorative elements spring from the 1880s or from some other period, yet none of them has anything to do with architecture.

Now, after the first victory of the early raw functionalism, we should be concerned with the development of the more vigorous and human side of functional architecture: a clear and functional frame around modern existence, created with new means; further development of tradition, perhaps, but not a return to forms past and gone. The barren qualities of functionalism came not from the relinquishment of the old, but rather from the failure to utilise in a sufficiently imaginative manner the possibilities of the new - new materials and construction, new social conditions.

Many factors will influence the architecture of the future. We must expect further technical development, perhaps encompassing possibilities yet dimly perceived. Sociological conditions have changed in many countries and will continue to do so, producing strong repercussions even in those countries where such changes have not yet occurred.

A building should be a shell around the life to be lived in it, a shell that will satisfy material as well as intellectual demands. The architect creates not life, but the conditions of life. Raymond Unwin once said: 'We cannot create life, but we can form the channels of life in such a way that the sources of life will flow into them of their own accord.'

Definitions are fluid and ideals vague in these postwar years. But, in view of the tactical position on the architectural front today, it is impolitic to emphasise the errors of functionalism. It is easy to retrogress; to retain and apply a new idea demands endurance. Today the building of houses is an intricate and troublesome business. Ever increasing demands for comfort and mechanical equipment challenge the architect; new modes of living complicate construction; ever-growing official intervention and restrictions limit planning; and everything is dominated by economy. Under these conditions, administration is assuming great importance; there will not be much room for free thought and for the idea that must be maintained. It is not enough to be receptive to outside influences; inner conviction must be allowed to grow and lead the way.

Reflections

For this section we invited reflections on aspects of Fisker's work from architects Job Floris and Tony Fretton, both of whom were already interested in Fisker prior to our research, and who were invaluable in supporting the production of this book.

The idea was not to provoke a discussion on Fisker's linear architectural influence, but rather to document a well known but little examined aspect of architectural production – that of reference, and the nuanced and occasionally contradictory way that the examples of figures from the past remain relevant and continue to shape architectural practice today.

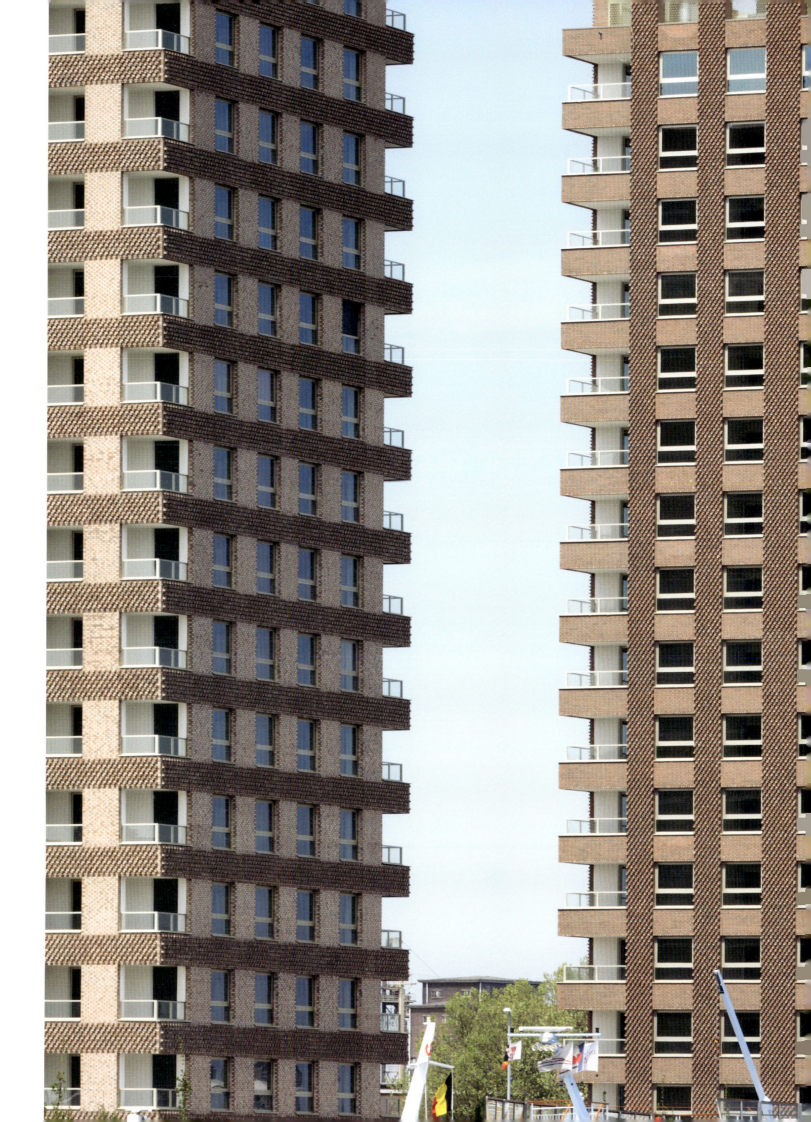

Westkaai towers. Photo: Peter Cook.

Response 1: Between Familiarity and Abstraction
Fisker in the Present Time

Tony Fretton

Facade-making is always about construction, use and representation; always constrained and always saying something about the times in which it was made. A creative practitioner will always view the work of another in terms of their own creative structure. In Fisker's work, which I have only lately begun to appreciate, I see a committed progressive, who was not a revolutionary like Le Corbusier, but a modernist in touch with social reality, and, perhaps most importantly for the present time, a progressive who easily maintained continuities with valuable social mores of Danish society and the history, form and landscape of the country's cities.

The work of my practice has come into being in a very different time, when the type of social and collective narratives that underpinned Fisker's work have been overwritten by individualism, deadening commodification and rhetoric. But in my experience as a social being and architect, I find that social narratives do, and in fact must exist simply in order for society to function. They are far less explicit than the grand narratives of modernism and more like fragmentary guiding impulses. Architect and writer William Mann places them in what he calls the 'unconscious collective'. I can see them in buildings and material objects that already exist, and can use what I see in the new buildings we make. I will illustrate this bydiscussing the design of facades, the most socially communicative parts of buildings, and show in detail how the use of brick in our building at Westkaai, in Antwerp, Belgium, has very different meaning to that in Fisker's Dronningegården housing.

The facade of the Dronningegården housing arcade takes its motifs from tradition – the vaulted masonry, the facade divided so as to be like a tall house, even a warehouse seen on the river, with the brickwork suggesting traditional masonry construction.

Abstract and rectangular, the brickwork of Westkaai is only decorative, while corner balconies give wide views of the harbour. The facade is uniform, the form of the tower subsuming the identities of specific apartments. The building presents an image that seeks to be liked – seen from the city as an icon, but not as demonstrative design. It is part of the visual fabric of the dockyard, its scale allowing it to engage with that of the passing boats, and the horizontality of the water in the dock.

Sometimes what makes a building special can only be described in simple or even banal terms. Brickwork you can lean out and touch, an irrational building that was somehow logical. But behind this is a serious wish, to make a building that people take seriously and like, that becomes a part of the city's landmarks.

Modernism presents a contrast – in many ways authoritarian, it adopted the mentality of science in insisting it knew best, something not always apparent at its time of construction but today increasingly loved for its enormous sociability. My work draws from modernisms abstraction, and the break from tradition it represents, but also offers space for humour, and the search for character in the making of a landmark.

Lisson Gallery facade, Tony Fretton Architects. Photo: Martin Charles.

Response 2: Two Tone

Job Floris

In several contemporary practices throughout Europe and beyond, the use of precedents and ancestors – a weaving- or reference-culture – has become part of the daily routine, as it has, of course, in ours. There is a group of good friends that regularly (metaphysically) visits the office, to take part in our discussions, showing off their design solutions for problems we have encountered that they have already struggled with and brought to a resolution ages ago. The constellation of this group changes constantly. New guests arrive at the table, while others fall silent and disappear. Some stay for a long time. The figure of Kay Fisker is among this group of good friends.

The idea of restrained experiment in his work is what intrigues me the most. It is an understanding that arose only slowly, after seeing many of Fisker's projects; a repeating set of themes became visible. While other Scandinavian architects, like Alvar Aalto, seemed to be very keen on their individual, artistic voice, I imagine Fisker to have been more restrained, dry, pragmatic. No moments of irony, but *sachlich* instead. His architecture appears to be rather conscious of its limited number of gestures and their relationship to the rationale of building systems. Being trained in the Beaux-Arts practice of Hack Kampmann, a rich foundation, he must have fully understood the arrival of new times with functionalism, New Objectivity and modernism.

Embracing the beauty and restrictions of masonry was one of the most successful of Fisker's strategies. This local and familiar material belonged to the contemporary conventions of the Danish building industry; the language of masonry was one which was widely understood among contractors and was economically viable. The use of brick immediately makes Fisker's buildings approachable, tangible, normal and familiar – even harmless, seemingly lacking the treat of the new and unknown. That ambition was played out on another level.

Fisker used a reduced palette of only two basic colours – yellow and red – which return in nearly every one of his projects, revealing an efficiency and a rather specific attitude towards experimentation as something that should take place within a strict bandwidth. These are merely variations – rather than a reinvention – of the vocabulary of the practice in each new project. The term 'two-tone' describes this coloured masonry, but also simultaneously refers to a specific type of ska music, a fast punk version of the slower Jamaican rocksteady genre. These musical 'variations on a theme' resonate somehow with Fisker's architecture. I'm not sure whether this is punk, though. Fisker fully engages with the banality of the everyday, by making his buildings simple and robust, bulky, almost dumb – and sometimes very boring due to their reductive nature. They do not contain a heavy load of gestures, an endless number of layers. They are not very eloquent, but direct and realistic; rather than communicating ten messages, he preferred to transmit no more than two.

Fisker embraced the camouflage of brick to create a free field for experiment, to explore new directions. Fisker's formal language was attuned to both classical and vernacular architecture, but only one at a time, making them appear in a rather reduced and tongue-in-cheek manner. Many of his projects made a rather relaxed use of conventional elements, such as tympanums, pitched roofs,

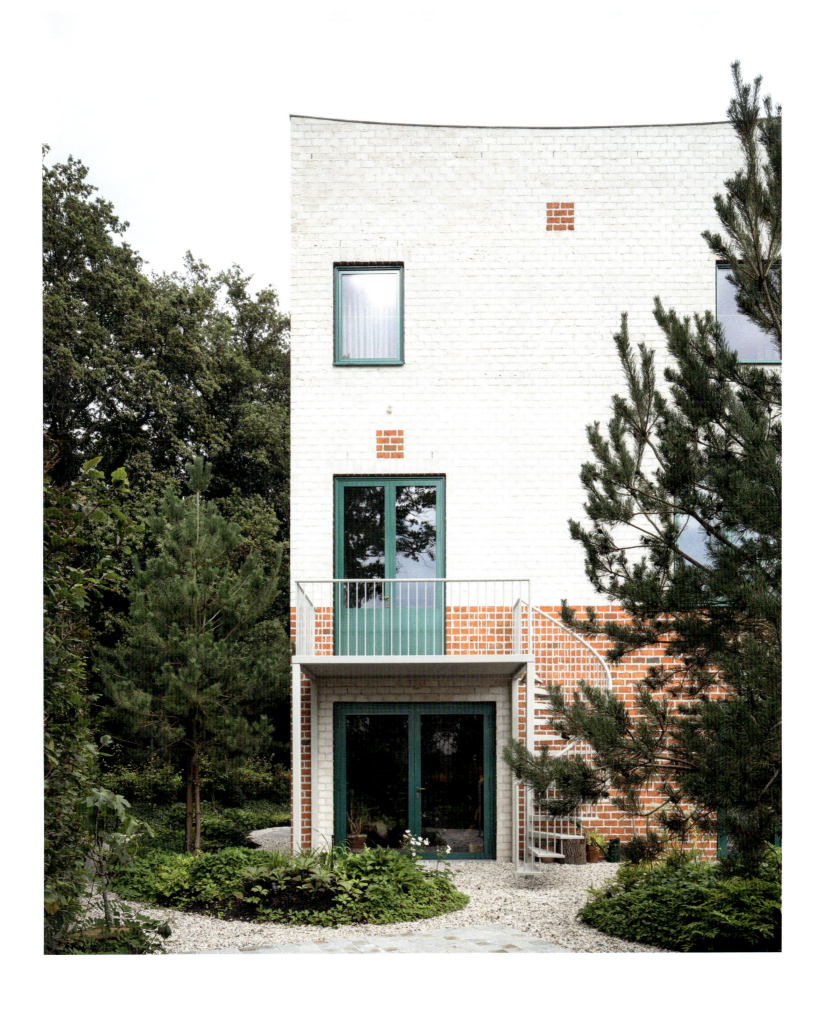

Landmark Nieuwe Bergen building by Monadnock Architects. Photo: Stijn Bollaert.

columns, corner rustications. Fisker felt free to make use of both ribbon windows and punched holes, without any dogma; all was possible within the rational of seriality and repetition.

Fisker's treatment of surfaces has a vague echo of the rustication of Leon Battista Alberti, treating the brick patterns as drawings – just a thin layer of meaning and gesture – though Alberti was probably seen as too frivolous for an architect like Fisker. Fisker created accents and slight gradients in colour, such as in the facades of the Dronningegården housing project in the centre of Copenhagen, from 1958, caused by patterns of crosses in the masonry. And at the Fogedgården housing project from 1945, in which coloured bands change to indicate an entrance. The masonry surfaces are charged with a layer of information, the weaving of patterns elevating the brickwork above common, plain masonry.

This specific treatment of masonry puts more emphasis on the jewels of a facade: the windows. After the masonry, Fisker used the window as the main tool of expression. There is virtually no layering in the elevations. He was aware of the tension between the surfaces of brick and the proportions and positioning of the windows, and dared to engage with the most direct and difficult approach; there is a single layer of brick and the rest of the narrative comes from the sole window, with no steps in between. In contrast, the Beaux-Arts vocabulary, the origin of Fisker's architecture, was based on an assemblage of elements and a large amount of layering. Even the Kollhoff Tower on Potsdamer Platz, in Berlin, designed by Hans Kollhoff in 1971 – an incredible building – was based on the idea of layering. Instead, Fisker's facade treatment has more resonance with the Italian architects Aldo Rossi and Giorgio Grassi. It is also worth mentioning the early works of the Swiss architect Roger Diener, who is heavily influenced by the approach of these two Italians and successfully takes these themes further.

Fisker's extravagance is found mainly in terms of scale, with twists in scale and the tweaking of a single element found in several of his projects. The steeply pitched roof between the two main long volumes of the Voldparken school, from 1957, for example, is interrupted by a high vertical tower as well as the head of one of the long volumes: a knot which is not simplified or austere at all. Instead, it is a most spectacular junction of roofs and vertical volumes, each fighting for dominance, while altogether being brought into an impressive self-conscious balance. The pitched roof is a starting point in many projects, immediately charging the project with a successful tension between figuration and abstraction, as the composition of the elevations are often rather abstract.

Fisker had a remarkable love for repetition. Was he just missing a notion of empathy? The facades of his large housing blocks with their shivering monumental repetition, such as Hornbækhus and the Glænøgaard, are impressive in their length and scale, and while normally one would feel the need to shorten these – or at least include some more variation over the lengths of these facades – Fisker did not. Instead, his empathy started at a much smaller scale. He skilfully added refinements to simple elements such as the frame of the window, entrance doors and corniches – the objects touched by hands on a daily basis. He created a subtle plasticity by positioning the framing around the windows slightly proud of the facade surface, or addressing entrances with a wider cement band. It is subtle ornamentation, a result of the logics of making, which mean these big blocks are digestible, in a beautiful way. Without doubt, Fisker had a talent for making his buildings urban, creating genuine 'street architecture': architecture forming streets and forming cities. He seemed very aware of the role he wanted his buildings to play – as a formal, tranquil backdrop forming an undisturbed public realm.

Fisker succeeded in stepping away from the abundance of gestures and symbols of his Beaux-Arts education, by embracing New Objectivity and rationalism, skilfully finding a new balance by bridging, rather than rejecting. It is Fisker's combination of austerity, calmness and slight boredom that makes his architecture so appealing: no fun, only dimmed extravagance in form, and we don't even miss these other ingredients. It is the reason we invite him to linger for so long around the table with us.

Response 3: Conversation and the Contingent

Andrew Clancy and Colm Moore

It may be reductive, but true nonetheless, to observe that there are architects who dream of a future, and work against the limits of their age to reach it; others yearn for a past, seek forms and languages no longer native to the way buildings are made in their time. Others still collapse into an unthinking delivery of a service to fit the commercial interests of their clients and practice. Kay Fisker had none of these tendencies. Instead, he was perhaps something rarer, what we might call a 'present tense architect' – aware of the limits and potentials of his time and his situation, and not constrained by habit or diverted by aspiration.

Fisker dominated his contemporary scene in Denmark but did not become canonical outside the country in the way his students Arne Jasobsen or Jørn Utzon did. Perhaps his language was too territorial, too rooted in the place – something not sought at that time. His role as a professor at the Royal Danish Academy's School of Architecture cemented this, and perhaps meant he inevitably became a reference in Denmark after his career had finished: not forgotten, but so intrinsic to the landscape as to be not worthy of extended study. Fisker himself lamented that he felt that he had never fulfilled his ambitions in architecture – a reference perhaps to the famous late work of Sigurd Lewerentz, the Swedish architect with whom Fisker had started his architectural career. When we came to Fisker's work many years after his passing, none of this was visible to us – only the work and its patient power.

We were drawn to Fisker initially as we taught, and we instructed the study that forms this book as research for our students, recognising its immediate value for our time: a lesson in care and keeping an eye on the limits and the simultaneous potential of an architect's agency. In the years since then perhaps the links have grown more evident. We have learned the necessity for open collaboration to engage with the challenges of our time and recognise a liberation here that was not part of our formal schooling, but which needs to be spoken about more often – the architect not as a brand but as a malleable participant. In recent years we have been commissioned to look at mass housing for the first time and now his memory in our minds is more direct, more urgent, as a living lesson talking to us about windows, about doors and stairs, about the practical and remarkable task of making a durable and robust habitat that might endure.

Fisker worked with what was available, from brick to timber windows. In each case the works he made were not rarefied in their conception or construction. It was in the assembly of ordinary things that their qualities as architecture were derived, their specialness not in any one part but in the sum of these parts. The repeated elements – if taken on their own – are well formed, but hardly worthy of investigation; it is in their assembly in a critical mass that something happens. Scale here does not become dehumanising, but rather becomes the essential component. The facades of Hornbækhus (1923) shimmer in plaster, glass and brick. Those of Vestersøhus (1935 and 1939), designed with C.F. Møller, ripple in a weave of balcony, recess, and open glass corners. The blocks of Aarhus University, also designed with C.F. Møller and Povl Stegmann in 1931, mutely hold the undulating ground with the inevitability of geology.

This calibration between the part and the whole is perhaps the most extraordinary aspect. It is in the overall order that it comes alive. These buildings possess a vital presence when seen from a distance, and yet act as well-judged background when much closer to them.

Almost all his buildings are still being used for their original intended uses, and even for their original clients. The housing has, if anything, only gained in desirability over time. Generations of families have grown up in his blocks, and they are burnished with the acts of maintenance and care that long-lived buildings accrete. There should not be anything unusual in this, perhaps – and yet there is. Special enough to become loved, not too special to be rendered unsympathetic to inhabitation and maintenance. Robust. The ideas that his buildings contained meant that each became an implied vernacular, the ideas capable of rapid assimilation by others. His vast courtyard gardens set a grain for Copenhagen housing for decades. The rhythm of corner bay window and recessed balcony established in Vestersøhus walked its way across numerous facades in Copenhagen and elsewhere – most known perhaps in the serrated facade of Hansaviertel in Berlin by Aalto (1957), but its generic presence in Danish housing is perhaps more valuable. Aarhus University was literally unfinished, and is still being added to years after the initial buildings were finished using the same details. The architecture is direct, informed by its making, and its intelligence is receptive to absorption by others.

Fisker's career coincided with a time of large-scale demographic change in Denmark: population growth and displacement caused by advances in technology, war and economic migration leading to a housing crisis comparable with our own time. In common with the time, Fisker's reading of practice was nimble, pliant and ever-changing. He collaborated freely, very rarely completing more than two or three projects with the same partner. In each conversation the work was pulled in a subtly different direction, and yet there is that consistent beat to it – an ability to engage with the individual and the collective equally, neither the gesture nor the order dominating. Economic, civic and humane at the same time.

Big Red, designed by Clancy Moore (Andrew Clancy and Colm Moore) with TAKA (Alice Casey and Cian Deegan) and Steve Larkin, for the London Festival of Architecture 2015, curated by Nathalie Weadick and Raymund Ryan. Photo: Andy Stagg.

Author Biographies

Andrew Clancy and Colm Moore are directors of Clancy Moore Architects in Dublin. Colm is also a senior lecturer at Queen's University, Belfast, where he directs the M.Arch programme. Andrew is Professor of Architecture at Kingston School of Art, London. Both completed PhDs with RMIT University, Melbourne, and both lecture and review work in numerous schools intenationally.

Job Floris is an architect and co-founder of MONADNOCK, a Rotterdam-based office for architecture, urbanism, interior design and research. He trained as an interior and furniture designer at the Royal Academy of Fine Arts and as an architect at the Rotterdam Academy of Architecture. Floris is head of the Master's Architecture course at the Rotterdam Academy of Architecture. He writes about architecture for various media and is a visiting lecturer at several architecture institutes.

Tony Fretton is founder, and now co-partner with James McKinney, of Tony Fretton Architects in London (founded 1982). Following international recognition of their buildings for the Lisson Gallery (in 1986 and 1992), the practice has consistently been short-listed in competitions for prestigious projects such as the Laban Centre for Dance (1997), the new 200,000sq-m headquarters for the Erste Bank Group in Vienna (2008), Fuglsang Art Museum in Southern Denmark (2008) and the new British Embassy in Warsaw (2009). Fretton recently finished his role as Professor and Chair of Architectural Design &Interiors at Technical University of Delft in the Netherlands, and was previously a visiting professor at EPFL Lausanne, the Berlage Institute Amsterdam, and the Graduate School of Design, Harvard, USA.

Martin Søberg is Associate Professor at the Institute of Architecture and Culture, Royal Danish Academy in Copenhagen. He is the author of *Kay Fisker: Works and Ideas in Danish Modern Architecture* (London: Bloomsbury, 2021).

Poul Sverrild is museum director at Forstadsmuseet in Hvidovre, Denmark. Following his MA in History from the University of Copenhagen (1981) he worked for the Danish National Archives (1982–4). After two years heading an interview project focused on memoirs of the 1920s and 1930s, he was employed as leader of Hvidovre Lokalarkiv (1985). Over the following decades he has headed the transformation of the small local historical archive into an urban ecomuseum covering the two suburban municipalities: Hvidovre and Brøndby.